OUTBACK STORIES
TRACKS FURTHER OUT

Published by Brolga Publishing Pty Ltd
ABN 46 063 962 443
PO Box 12544, A'Beckett St, VIC, 8006, Australia
email: markzocchi@brolgapublishing.com.au

All rights reserved. No part of this publication may be reproduced, stored in a retrieval system or transmitted in any form or by any means electronic, mechanical, photocopying, recording or otherwise without prior permission from the publisher.

All efforts have been made to contact the copyright owners of images and any omissions will be corrected in future reprints.

Copyright 2015 © Ian Ferguson

National Library of Australia Cataloguing-in-Publication entry:

Ferguson, Ian, 1941-
Outback stories : tracks further out / Ian Ferguson.
9781925367058 (pbk.)
Country life—Australia—Anecdotes.
Frontier and pioneer life—Australia—History.
Australia—Rural conditions—History.
306.0994

Printed in Australia
Cover by Wanissa Somsuphangsri
Typeset by Esther van Doornum

OUTBACK STORIES
TRACKS FURTHER OUT

Ian Ferguson

CONTENTS

1. Our First Explorers 1
2. Lifestyles of Pioneer Families 31
3. Memorable Outback Characters 53
4. Heroes of the Outback 75
5. Outstanding Women of the Outback 91
6. High Achiever on Tracks Further Out 123
7. Outback Writers, Singers, Artists and Actors .. 165
8. Outback Tragedies 201
9. Disasters and Mysteries of the Outback....... 227

Bibliography 257
Index 258

CHAPTER ONE:
OUR FIRST EXPLORERS

*"Ghostly lines of scrub at daybreak—
dusty day break in the drought—
And a lonely swagman tramping, on the
track to further out."*
("The Last Review", Henry Lawson)

William Dampier

The first European settlements in New Holland (the original name of Australia) were all English colonies. This is surprising, as the Dutch mariners Willem Janz and Dirk Hartog both sighted the coastline of this isolated continent decades before any known English explorer landed on our shores.

The first known English visitor was William Dampier, who criticised the future potential of this virtually unknown land. He noted that the north-west area where he landed showed little evidence of surface water supplies, and

Captain James Cook

no fruit or berry trees grew in this arid environment. Furthermore, the forthright buccaneer declared, the few natives he observed were" the most miserable people on Earth, who differ little from brutes."

Before Dampier's 1688 expedition, a few romantics believed that an undiscovered and potentially opulent "El Dorado" existed somewhere in the South Seas. However all interest about settling New Holland evaporated, after Dampier made his scathing opinions known. Ironically he landed close to the mineral rich Pilbara area of Australia, which now yields lucrative quantities of iron ore to domestic and global markets.

Nearly a century after Dampier landed, James Cook was commissioned by the Royal Geographic Society and British Admiralty to make observations from Tahiti about a transit of the planet Venus. Cook's epic voyage in the "Endeavour" led to a renewed interest being shown in New Holland after he sailed along the previously unknown east coast in 1770.

It was a crucial mission, as this leg of Cook's long voyage would ascertain whether or not a habitable "Great Southland" existed. Fortunately the accomplished mariner discovered a much more luxuriant part of the continent "where most sorts of grains, fruits and roots of every kind would flourish". Cook anchored the "Endeavour" at four separate vantage points along the impressively fertile east coast, much of which he named New South Wales (NSW).

Captain Cook was much more tolerant and understanding about the indigenous people than previous European explorers. He observed that "the earth and sea of their own accord furnishes them with all (they require); they covet not magnificent houses, and live in a warm climate (where they) have very little need for clothing...They did not value anything we gave them. They (are already) provided with the necessities of life".

Captain Joseph Banks

Joseph Banks, an eminent botanist, was an influential member of Cook's expedition. Three years after their epic South Seas voyage, Banks recommended to authorities in England, that a colony be established at Botany Bay, where Cook first landed during his east coast voyage of discovery. Banks' views about the creation of a new permanent settlement were warmly received, as England faced a social welfare crisis in regard to their grossly overcrowded prisons.

The harsh criminal justice system of the time created an unwanted surplus of prisoners. All available English jails were markedly over-populated, and the rotting hulks of ships left abandoned in the Thames River had become make-shift prisons. By 1783, the overcrowding of penal institutes became more serious, after the newly independent American colonies banned the importation of convict labour.

Another "colony of thieves" was urgently needed, so in August 1786 it was announced from London's Home Office, that Botany Bay would become the site for a new convict settlement. Arthur Phillip, who became the first Governor of NSW, was advised to begin the new colony there. He was instructed to use convict labour to cultivate the land for grain crops and other plant foods, and to maintain acceptable religious principles and lawful order in the new community. He was also issued with the challenge of gaining the trust and affection of the indigenous population. These lofty aspirations may have seemed reasonable when Phillip first raised the Union Jack over the first settlement at Port Jackson on 26th January 1788, a date which is now celebrated as Australia Day.

However, the ambitious goals formulated in far off England were doomed to fail. It was never realistic to believe that indolent criminals from the London slums would become diligent and skilful farmers in such an unfamiliar landscape; the seasons were directly opposite to their northern hemisphere experience. Furthermore, the convict labour force did not react well to the incessant heat, the stinging ants, or to tilling the back-breaking infertile soil for much needed crops.

Australia's first settlement at Port Jackson

From the outset, many of the local indigenous people were hostile towards the white invaders. At the first flag raising ceremony to launch the new colony, an angry crowd of aborigines yelled abuse at the European newcomers. All efforts to recruit them into the workforce were resisted, and poor early harvests rapidly decreased available food stocks. Strict rationing of food was imposed, but by 1790 the struggling colony faced starvation.

Fortunately, the arrival of the supply ship "Lady Julianna" provided temporary relief, but by then it was clear to Governor Phillip that the colony was in dire straits. Fertile land needed to be found in the interior of the continent, which could be farmed by free settlers. Motivated newcomers were also earmarked to build new roads, bridges and public buildings, which were urgently needed in the growing colony.

The first settlement lurched closer to collapse after Phillip returned to England in 1792, and it wasn't until Governor Lachlan Macquarie arrived in 1809 that the struggling colony of NSW began to prosper. "Macquarie the builder" encouraged early explorers to find a way over the seemingly impenetrable Blue Mountains, in the hope that better grazing lands would be discovered for the many eager free settlers arriving from the British Isles.

CROSSING THE BLUE MOUNTAINS

Some historical researchers credit either a convict or a Frenchman for being the first Europeans to cross the Blue Mountains, but to this day neither John Wilson or Francis Barrallier are commonly regarded as being the first to record this breakthrough achievement. Cricket fans and others will insist that it was "LBW" (Lawson, Blaxland and Wentworth) who made the crossing, which was a landmark achievement. It finally allowed the overcrowded and struggling colony to expand across the vast, fertile slopes that lay to the west of Sydney.

William Lawson, Gregory Blaxland and William Wentworth pursued a new tactic when they began their challenging expedition from Emu Plains on 11th May 1813. Since 1790, various escaping convicts and adventurers had attempted to follow rivers through the mountains, only to frequently find their journey blocked by rapids, sheer cliffs and gorges. The three young explorers decided instead to follow the mountain ridges in their attempt to cross the difficult mountain barrier, and this strategy proved successful.

The expedition lasted 21 days, but, after coping with inadequate food supplies, thick undergrowth, sickness and the ever present threat of aboriginal attacks, the intrepid trio conquered the rugged terrain. A way through the Blue Mountains had been found, and it took Lawson, Blaxland and Wentworth only five days to return in triumph to Sydney Town.

Six months later George Evans reached the position where Bathurst now stands, and in 1814 William Cox used a band of 30 convicts to build a road linking Penrith to Bathurst through the previously impenetrable mountain barrier.

New opportunities now beckoned in the west, and various

future explorers, overlanders and settlers played a prominent part in developing the vast interior of this ancient and challenging land.

Left to right: William Lawson, Gregory Blaxland and William Wentworth

Hamilton Hume

NEW PASTORAL LAND BETWEEN SYDNEY AND PORT PHILLIP

In 1824 Governor Brisbane invited Hamilton Hume to join former English sea captain William Hovell, in an ambitious expedition that would commence at Lake George (near present day Canberra) and finish at Spencer Gulf, in what is now South Australia. The 27-year-old Hume, who became the first prominent Australian born explorer, had engaged in exploration activities near his birthplace of Parramatta since the age of 17 and was well regarded in the colony.

The pair led a party of 16 men and carried enough supplies to last 16 weeks. Early in their journey flood waters from the Murrumbidgee River forced them to use their carts as boats, before they reached the foothills of the Australian Alps. On 16th November they discovered the Hume River (later re-named the Murray River) at a site where the border city of Albury now stands. There Hovell carved his name on the "Hovell Tree", which remains an historical landmark to this day.

The party then travelled south-west through thickly wooded country that was rich in agricultural potential. After viewing Mt Buffalo, they ascended the Eastern Highlands near Mt Macedon and crossed the Werribee River, before reaching the ocean at what they believed was Westernport Bay. In actuality, it was "Jilong" (later named Geelong) and the area of water became Corio Bay, which was part of Port Phillip Bay. By then their supplies were dwindling, so by 18th January 1825 they had returned to Lake George.

Their three month expedition was significant, as Hume and Hovell discovered much land between Sydney and Melbourne that was well suited to pastoral development. Hamilton Hume later joined Charles Sturt in his 1828 expedition to the Darling River area, but soon after declining health forced him to retire to his property near Yass. He later died at Goulburn in 1872, three years before his older colleague Hovell passed away.

The Murray River, originally named the Hume River

THE SEARCH FOR AN INLAND SEA

Charles Sturt

Charles Sturt was an intrepid explorer who made four attempts to discover what the early settlers craved for—an inland sea, similar to the Great Lakes system of North America. This precious water would be utilised to irrigate future crops and pasture land in the undiscovered interior of the continent.

The Indian born army captain arrived in NSW from England in 1827, and soon afterwards Sturt joined forces with Hamilton Hume to map the course of the Macquarie River. The explorers then moved on to the Darling River, where a terrible drought convinced them that an inland sea did not exist in that area of the colony.

Two years later Sturt investigated the course of the Murrumbidgee River, on what proved to be a highly dangerous journey. During the arduous voyage, where they alternated between sailing and rowing in a very basic boat, there were treacherous rocks and trees hidden below the surface. Finally they came across another huge expanse of water, which proved to be the Murray River. A friendly group of aborigines helped them to avoid violence from a more hostile group of indigenous locals, before they discovered the lower reaches of the Darling River.

By then Sturt had proved that the main

rivers flowing west from the Sydney area, turned south towards the ocean instead of maintaining a course that ended in an inland sea, closer to the centre of the continent. On 4th February, 1830, the exploratory group reached the mouth of the Murray at Lake Alexandrina, from where the meandering river flowed into the sea.

Unfortunately, when they rowed back to their base camp on the Murrumbidgee, they found the site had been abandoned. By then the river was in flood and food supplies were low. Sturt rested at Narrandera, and sent Hopkinson and Mullholland off to discover the rest of the exploration party, and bring back vital food supplies. After this gruelling expedition, a noticeably weakened Sturt suffered blindness for a month; he continued to suffer vision problems for the remainder of his life. Sturt's findings from this challenging trip had significant future benefits, as it proved a colony could be established at a site that later became Adelaide.

In 1838 Sturt drove a herd of cattle from Sydney to Adelaide. There he was appointed Surveyor-General and later became Registrar-General of South Australia.

Sturt led a fourth expedition, when he attempted to reach the centre of the continent. By then he believed that no inland sea existed, but the now 50-year-old veteran trailblazer hoped to discover significant lakes in the interior. At Broken Hill he failed to recognise the rich mineral wealth for which the area later became famous. However, further north (near present day Milparina) Sturt discovered deep under-ground water supplies.

Then, for nearly six months, the expedition virtually ground to a halt because of the intense heat and scarcity of drinking water. Finally heavy rain saved the desperate group, though scurvy killed some of his team. After crossing they encountered a vast barren area that they named Sturt's Stony Desert. From there the weary travellers retreated to the relative comfort of Fort Grey.

It was 17 months before the exploration party returned to civilization, and by then a very ill Sturt had to be transported in a dray. Charles Sturt was awarded a gold medal in Adelaide for his significant exploration achievements, and in his later years he returned to England, where he died in 1869.

THE KNIGHT OF ALL EXPLORERS

Sir Thomas Mitchell

Colonel Sir Thomas Mitchell was not only the first Australian explorer to receive a knighthood; he was also arguably the last person of note to challenge an adversary to a duel. (Fortunately the shot Mitchell allegedly fired passed through his enemy's hat).

Mitchell was a controversial figure. His short temper was legendary, but this multi-talented man was a skilled geologist, botanist, painter, poet and explorer. His legacy in regard to indigenous Australians is not as laudible. Often he did not treat them with kindness or respect, and it is rumoured that he shot and killed many aborigines during his excursions into the outback.

In 1831 Mitchell travelled into the north-west region of NSW and discovered the lower courses of the Peel, Namoi, Gwydir and Dumaresqu Rivers. He also reached the Upper Darling. Two years later the tireless explorer investigated the land between the Bogan and Macquarie Rivers, and in 1835 he traced the Darling River a further 300 miles out from the inland town of Bourke. A year later the course of the Lachlan River was followed, and Mitchell also reached the Murrumbidgee, the Murray and the junction of the Murray and Darling Rivers. The explorer then returned south along the Murray and discovered the

Avoca and Glenelg Rivers, before reaching the coast near Cape Northumberland.

The ill-fated Edward Kennedy (who was later murdered by north Queensland aborigines) was his exploration companion when Mitchell discovered the Warrego, Belgardo and Barcoo Rivers. However, his quest to find a river running into the Gulf of Carpentaria proved unsuccessful.

Overall, Sir Thomas Mitchell's four major explorations opened up rich pastoral areas in Central Queensland and vast areas of south-eastern Australia, including southern Victoria.

A sketch of the Salvator River by Sir Thomas Mitchell, c1846

INTO THE NEVER-NEVER

John McDouall Stuart migrated to Australia from Scotland at the age of 23. Six years later he joined Charles Sturt on a journey towards the centre of the continent, before earning his living as a surveyor for the next 12 years.

John McDouall Stuart

Stuart then explored country around Coober Pedy, before investigating Eyre Peninsula areas around Streaky Bay and Port Lincoln. Stuart's achievements on this journey were highly acclaimed in Adelaide, as approximately 40,000 acres of prime sheep grazing country was discovered.

After travelling north in 1859, Stuart found the impressive McDonnell Ranges. Then, on 22nd March (when he sighted Central Mt Stuart) the determined explorer believed that he had reached the very centre of the continent. Stuart then travelled on to Tennant Creek, which was about 200 miles further on from previously explored country to the north.

Towards the end of the following year, the South Australian Government financed a Stuart led expedition, which would compete with the Victorian sponsored Burke and Wills initiative. The aim of both exploration groups was to become the first Europeans to traverse Australia from south to north, but Stuart was forced to return after reaching Sturt's Plain. In 1861 the ubiquitous Stuart again gained government funding in another attempt to cross the continent. On this occasion he stopped at Daly Waters before finally reaching the Indian Ocean.

Three years later a white haired, exhausted and nearly blind Stuart visited his native Scotland, where he died in hospital at the age of 52. By then he had allegedly become a controversial and lonely man, who had reportedly developed a drinking problem.

After his death, John McDouall Stuart's exploration discoveries became more significant when the Port Augusta to Darwin Overland Telegraph was constructed, on a route that had been originally established by the trail-blazing Scot. In more modern times it was named the Stuart Highway, and it remains an important arterial road in the Australian outback.

John McDouall Stuart planting the Union Jack
on Central Mount Stuart, 1860

CROSSING THE NULLABOR

It took nearly five arduous months for Edward John Eyre (and his loyal aboriginal companion Wylie) to cross much of Australia from east to west. Their testing journey between Adelaide and Albany, transported them across the treeless Nullarbor Plain and became one of the most dramatic expeditions in Australian history.

Edward John Eyre

Edward John Eyre arrived in Australia from Britain as a 17-year-old. For some time he was involved in droving and exploration excursions around NSW, South Australia and Western Australia. In 1839 he attempted to open up a viable stock route to the centre of the continent, but was forced to return after reaching the appropriately named Mt Hopeless.

A year later Eyre was appointed leader of an expedition that sought to establish a viable transport connection between South Australia and Western Australia. It was anticipated that valuable farming land would be discovered on the journey, and that an overland cattle route would be established. On route, a government funded supply ship would replenish their food supplies at Spencers Gulf.

By the time the group reached the now named Eyre Peninsula, they were already experiencing hardships. Lack of water forced Eyre to keep only Baxter, Wylie, two other aboriginals and himself in the exploration party, together with 11 pack horses and six sheep.

Conditions were almost unbearable. On the 1,300 kilometre journey across the arid Nullarbor Plain, water supplies rapidly diminished. Some friendly indigenous people on the Great Australian Bight showed them how to dig for water in the sand dunes, but the small group still faced incredible hardships. Relief was briefly found when wells were discovered at Eucla, but six days later their existing water supplies had been consumed and their horses had perished. Eyre and Baxter both became ill after being forced to eat a sick horse.

When the outback winter began, they had only reached the half-way point of their arduous journey. By then, two aboriginal members of the group were not coping well with the bitterly cold early morning and evening conditions. Their discontent finally flared into violent rebellion.

One night they shot Baxter dead and disappeared into the darkness with most of the camp supplies and firearms. The rocky terrain prevented Eyre and Wylie from burying their dead comrade. They were finally forced to leave his body wrapped in a blanket, before resuming their journey.

The pair trudged through the desolate landscape for another month, and at one stage existed without water for seven days. Kangaroos were killed for food, and a desperate Eyre even ate a dead penguin he found on a beach. In June 1841 their luck changed, when a French whaling ship was sighted close to shore. Meeting the whalers proved to be the explorers' salvation, as the two men regained their strength and health during their two weeks of recuperation with their rescuers.

In July a refreshed Eyre and Wylie continued on through heavy rain and cold conditions to Albany. Their epic journey had taken four and a half months and Wylie elected to settle in Albany after he received a government pension.

Eyre was presented with a gold medal from the Royal Geographical Society. He then commenced a successful but sometimes controversial public life. In 1846 he became Lieutenant-Governor of New Zealand, and he also served as governor in various areas of the Caribbean, where he faced political turmoil in Jamaica.

The situation there became violent and Eyre was forced to forcefully suppress a rebellion. Two local indigenous men were flogged and later killed during the uprising and George William Gordon (a mixed race Jamaican politician) was executed. Eyre was subsequently charged twice with murder, but on both occasions legal proceedings did not proceed further.

Edward John Eyre was aged 86 when he died in 1901.

Edward John Eyre's expedition

VANISHED WITHOUT TRACE

Ludwig Leichardt

He was a Prussian naturalist and explorer who made two important journeys of discovery in northern and central Australia. However, when he was later pursuing an ambitious plan to cross the country from the eastern seaboard to the south-west coast of Western Australia, Ludwig Leichardt vanished in the "never-never".

Leichardt was a young boy when he immigrated to Australia from England with his family, and in 1844-45 he embarked on his first major expedition. The enthusiastic young man trekked nearly 5,000 kilometres when he explored the territory between the Darling Downs in southern Queensland and Port Essington on the Gulf of Carpentaria. A hero's welcome awaited Leichardt when he returned in triumph.

A little over a year later, Leichardt raised the bar of expectation considerably, when he began an ambitious excursion that commenced again on the Darling Downs and aimed to conclude at Perth on the other side of the continent. Heavy rains, bouts of malaria and famine intervened before they had travelled 1,000 kilometres, and the struggling explorers were forced to return home. Once again the scholarly young man received praise for his exploratory achievements.

In March 1848 the rural settlement of Condamine became the start of another Leichardt expedition, which he hoped would conclude in the Swan River region of Western Australia. The 35-year-old explorer was last sighted on 3rd April 1848 at McPherson's Station on the Darling Downs. Soon after departing further inland, however, Ludwig Leichardt disappeard.

Clues about his ultimate fate have been inconclusive. Four years after Leichardt vanished a tree marked with the letter "L" was found near an old campsite on the Flinders River near the Gulf of Carpentaria. Then, in 1896, another expedition found an iron tent peg, the lid of a tin, a match box and part of a saddle in the forbidding Gibson and Great Sandy Desert areas of outback Australia. In more recent times, an authenticated tiny brass plate bearing Leichardt's name was discovered near Sturt Creek on the Western Australian and Northern Territory border.

The mystery about the explorer's fate has fascinated generations of Australians, including the acclaimed author Patrick White.

The reclusive White, who in 1973 became the first Australian recipient of the Nobel Prize for Literature, immortalised Leichardt in his highly praised novel, *Voss*. This book also won the inaugural Miles Franklin Literary Award in 1957.

"The Starting of the Leichardt Search" by Frederick Grosse

VIOLENCE IN THE OUTBACK

Edmund Kennedy was aged 22 when he arrived from England in 1840 and became the Assistant Surveyor of NSW. Luminary explorer Sir Thomas Mitchell soon became somewhat of a mentor to the young man. In exploration journeys around northern NSW and inland Queensland, Kennedy was part of the exploratory group that discovered the Thompson and Barcoo Rivers, as well as Coopers Creek.

In December 1848 Edmund Kennedy was exploring around Cape York Peninsula when he was speared to death by a hostile group of local aborigines. The unfortunate victim was only about 40 kilometres from a supply ship when he was attacked and his loyal indigenous companion, Jacky Jacky, guarded and comforted Kennedy before he died. Fortunately, Jacky Jacky survived the ordeal and found safe refuge in the waiting vessel.

THE DISASTROUS BURKE AND WILLS EXPERIMENT

In 1860 Victorian colonial authorities approved an ambitious plan to explore the length of Australia from south to north. The idea was enthusiastically embraced by the general public, some of whom held hopes that an inland sea was still waiting to be discovered. Generous amounts of money were made available to finance the expedition, and the handsome sum of two thousand pounds was offered for those who succeeded in crossing the continent.

Twenty-eight horses and wagons, 24 camels and numerous beads and trinkets for indigenous populations they would encounter were purchased, and two years of food supplies was allocated for the expedition. These thorough preparations should have guaranteed a successful outcome. However, the plan was a disaster, largely because authorities chose the wrong man to lead the group.

It still remains a mystery why Robert O'Hara Burke was placed in command of an expedition into unknown territory. It was rumoured that he frequently became lost, when he previously served as a policeman in the Beechworth area. Burke was also known to be an impatient and impetuous man. Questions could have been asked about the 38-year-old's emotional maturity, given that he had bequeathed all his worldly possessions to a 15-year-old actress,

Above: Robert O'Hara Burke
Bellow: William John Wills

whom he had been unsuccessfully courting.

Any misgivings about leadership were not evident, however, when a large cheering crowd and a brass band provided a stirring farewell for Burke, his surveyor-astronomer William John Wills and the other 14 members of the 1860 exploratory team, when the party departed through the north gate of Melbourne's Royal Parade. Unfortunately Burke's rash decision making soon became a problem.

At the outset it seemed a reckless decision to take on such a major expedition in the height of the outback summer. At the time a rival South Australian expedition (under the leadership of John McDouall Stuart) had been formed. This rivalry for trans-Australian honours may have been the catalyst for Burke's risky decision to travel during the hottest time of the year. His quest for faster travel may explain an early decision to dump precious food supplies, and when he reached Menindie, he impatiently left half of the original exploration group behind. Consequently, when the next leg of the journey was taken to Coopers Creek, only eight men continued with the expedition.

Public funeral of Burke and Wills

Wright was left in charge of those who remained in Menindie, and he was ordered to follow on within a few days.

By mid-December, six weeks after departing from Menindie, the unreliable Wright had not arrived with his support team. Consequently Burke decided to have Wills, King and Gray accompany him on the arduous final leg of the journey to the Gulf of Carpentaria, while the other four stayed behind at the Coopers Creek depot. Finally, on 16th February 1861, the exhausted group, who survived stifling heat, frequent thunderstorms and boggy conditions, etched their way into Australian history records—they became the first European explorers to cross Australia from south to north.

Even greater problems confronted them on the return journey. By then food stocks were dangerously low and Gray had begun stealing their meagre supplies. Burke savagely beat the man for this serious indiscretion, but the sick and exhausted Gray became too weak to walk and he soon died from starvation and exposure. A further precious day was lost while the surviving members buried their dead comrade and it wasn't until 21st April that the exhausted trio staggered into the depot at Coopers Creek.

Their relief quickly turned to despair as they found the camp deserted. A frantic search revealed the message "Dig 3 Feet NW" cut into a tree, and their digging uncovered welcome food supplies as well as a short written note, which provided disappointing news. The support group, after waiting for four months for their arrival, had only departed hours before Burke, Wills and King finally reached the depot.

Despite their poor physical condition, Burke decided to lead his comrades to the nearest cattle station, which was a further 240 kilometres from Coopers Creek. Again the desperate men lacked the "Midas touch" as Brahe, the leader of the group that had recently waited at Coopers Creek, unexpectedly returned to the depot after the weary trio set off for the cattle station. Burke left no evidence of their brief stay, so when Brahe found the refuge area abandoned he assumed that Burke's group were either dead or lost, so he left no horses or food supplies before departing again. In a further cruel ironic twist, the ill fated Burke Wills and King soon abandoned the long trek to the cattle station and returned to the relative safety of the depot.

At Coopers Creek the trio actually survived for several weeks on nardoo seeds, fish and other food provided by friendly indigenous people. However, by the end of June both Burke and Wills had died, so when a rescue party arrived soon after only King was alive. His survival was largely due to the nurturing skills of local aborigines.

Burke, Brahe and Wright all made crucial leadership errors of judgement during this ambitious expedition, which resulted in three brave men suffering horrible and lonely deaths in Australia's vast outback. It was the country's worst exploration disaster and human error was largely to blame

THE BARON OF THE WEST

Baron John Forrest, who finally received his Royal honour in the year he died, was one of Western Australia's high achievers. He became an esteemed explorer, his state's Premier, a Federal politician and Cabinet Minister and Australia's first native born peer.

Baron John Forrest

Some observers later claimed that John Forrest's most notable contributions were all realised during his youth. One especially trenchant critic later dismissed him as being "a successful political power broker in a small colony… (but) in wealthy old age he appeared (to be) more concerned with Empire and wealth, than the betterment of society". This appears to be a harsh assessment when John Forrest's many achievements are listed.

Forrest was born in Bunbury in 1843, and at the age of 26 he led a search party through unexplored parts of Western Australia (WA) in a vain bid to locate the lost explorer, Ludwig Leichardt. A year later he followed and surveyed the route that Edward John Eyre and Wylie followed across the Nullarbor 30 years previously. Then, in 1874 he led an exploration through arid country east of Geraldton, until the Overland Telegraph line was reached in South Australia.

John Forrest became Premier of WA in 1890 and for the next decade he presided over a period of significant economic growth.

After gold was discovered in 1892 and 1893 at Coolgardie and Kalgoorlie respectively, the state enjoyed an economic boom. However, the absence of a reliable and economic water supply to the Eastern Goldfields area was a massive problem and cartage by rail very expensive. Under the strong leadership of Premier Forrest, a solution was found.

Designer engineers proposed a scheme which would deliver abundant supplies of water at a cheap price. The main source of supply would be the Mundaring Dam near Perth, and a project incorporating this water source was proposed by Forrest to the Western Australian Parliament in 1896. Sceptics said it would never work and that the state would be left with huge debts once gold supplies ran out. Allegations of corruption and misdemeanours were levelled at the administration, and C.Y. O'Connor, one of the project's main designers, committed suicide during the crisis. A subsequent inquiry later cleared his name.

Finally steel pipes carried the precious fluid on a 550 kilometre journey through some of the most arid country on the planet. Eight pumping stations and two small holding dams serviced the project and in 1903 the world's largest fresh water pipeline was completed. Today the project caters for over 100,000 people in more than 30,000 households as well as the water needs of mines, farms and other enterprises.

During his time as Premier, Forrest believed that WA would benefit most by separating political ties with other states. However, in later years he embraced the Federation concept and he played a significant role in the "Yes" vote prevailing at the turn of the century.

During his term as Premier, Forrest oversaw other vital projects. He encouraged the dredging of Fremantle harbour, and was also instrumental in over a 1,000 kilometres of railway track being laid across the vast state.

The most significant transport achievement for the West, was the construction of the Trans Australian Railway, which crosses the vast Nullarbor Plain from Port Augusta in South Australia to Kalgoorlie in WA.

When the Federation of the Australian states was achieved in 1901, WA was very isolated from the rest of the country. Sea journeys were the only transport possibility and passenger ship trips were time consuming, inconvenient and often uncomfortable.

One of the Federation pre-requisites for WA, was a federally funded rail link with the rest of the continent. A 1909 survey initially proposed the linkage of Port Augusta to Tarcoola. It was estimated that the approximate cost of this could reach the equivalent of ten million dollars. Work continued on the vital rail link during World War I and during the construction period the "Tea and Sugar" train carried necessary supplies to isolated work sites and settlements along the transport route.

Overall it was a very time consuming project. The two halves of rail met on 17th October 1917, but the standard gauge needs were not addressed until 1970. The completed Trans Australian Railway covered 1,692.60 kilometres, which was slightly less than the predicted distance.

No natural water supplies are available along its route, and before a pipeline supply from near Perth was completed, approximately half the loading capacity of freight trains was devoted to water. The Trans Australian Railway also contains the world's longest stretch of dead straight railway track—a 478 kilometre stretch between Ooldea and Loongara.

In 1901 Forrest was elected as the Federal Member for Swan and at various times over the next 17 years he served in Government Ministry positions as Postmaster-General, the

Minister for Defence and Treasurer.

John Forrest died in 1918 at the age of 75.

Construction of the Trans Australian Railway

CHAPTER TWO:

LIFESTYLES OF PIONEER FAMILIES

> *"Back in the early fifties,*
> *Dim through the mists of years,*
> *By the bush-grown strand of a wild, strange land*
> *We entered—the pioneers..."*
> *(Frank Hudson)*

The early pioneers, lured by the potential wealth of acquired land, soon followed the first Australian explorers into often formidable landscapes. Their hopes were sometimes thwarted, initially because of conflicting attitudes between themselves and local indigenous people over land ownership issues.

The newcomers arrived with firm beliefs that the land was purely an economic resource, which they could utilise for their own benefit, through either leased or freehold tenure, that was sanctioned by the British Crown.

In Britain's other oversesas colonies, some attempt at fair dealings were often negotiated with the local indigenous people. However, in Australia "Terra Nullius" applied, which effectively meant that, in the eyes of the law, Australia was unoccupied before Europeans first arrived on the continent. This draconian piece of legislation shamefully remained in existence until the historic "Mabo case" of 1992, when the High Court of Australia ruled that Murray Island in the Torres Strait was subject to native title.

The perceived right of Europeans to annex land for their exclusive use, resulted from completely different cultural attitudes. In the view of new settlers, aborigines were not using the land, as this largely nomadic group of indigenous people grew no crops, raised no domestic animals for food supplies, and constructed few permanent dwellings. Consequently the landscape remained uncultivated and unused, which, in the view of the new settlers, was a wasted resource. They failed to understand the spiritual significance that the land held for these people, whose traditional beliefs remain unmatched in longevity by any other group on the planet.

Traditionally for indigenous Australians, the land was formed by their ancestral forbears in the ancient Dreamtime, a spiritual concept which embraces their past, present and future obligations. They have a "oneness" with nature and the land itself is a direct link between all living things, and the eternal, mythical world of their spirit ancestors. It could be said, that in spiritual terms, land has the same significance to aboriginal people, that the Bible or Koran has to followers of Christian and Muslim faiths.

Various clans, bands and sub-tribes of indigenous Australians were designated by Dreamtime oral traditions to be the custodians of sometimes thousands of kilometres of virgin land. Around 20-50 different headsmen had overall authority over their allocated plot, and they were responsible for its continued existence. Such decrees were communicated through special ceremonies and totemic relationships with native flora and fauna.

This unique emotional response to the land was completely at odds with the capitalistic views that the first European settlers brought with them. The idea that any individual could have exclusive use of the land for their own purposes, was completely foreign to traditional indigenous beliefs.

> *"...and we blazed the track, and fought with the black*
> *So that ye may inherit the land."*
> *(Frank Hudson)*

There were indeed violent conflicts between some aboriginal groups and early settlers. In October 1835 ten European men and women were slaughtered at Hornet Creek Station in outback Queensland by a group of male members of the local Jiman tribe. A series of alleged sexual assaults against indigenous women, perpetrated by the 22-year-old son of the late European station owner, apparently triggered the after-dark massacre. Two days later an angry vigilante group of Europeans enacted revenge, killing five aborigines among a group they found near the homestead.

In June 1838, at Myall creek in north-west NSW, approximately 30 aboriginal women and children were roped together and either shot or decapitated by a group of European men. A large funeral pyre removed much of the evidence, but on this occasion the culprits were apprehended by authorities, and seven of those found guilty were subsequently executed. Queensland continued to record the worst number of racial fatalities and by 1866 the majority of the 600 Europeans and 15,000 aborigines murdered nationally in violent altercations, had been slain in that state.

Pioneer women in particular feared for their personal safety in isolated outback areas, especially if they were forced to cope on their own when their husbands worked far from home. In the early 20th century, Evelyn "Evie" Maunsell, recalled the night she hid under her bed at Mt Mulgrave Station, when five spear-carrying Mitchell River warriors invaded the house when her husband Charlie was absent. It is little wonder she feared for her life. Previously hostile "myalls" (local wild aborigines) had speared a neighbour to death, shortly before Evie arrived at the homestead as a new bride.

Tensions simmered between the early settlers at the station and the local indigenous people, after Paddy Callaghan, the previous property manager, reportedly raped and murdered several local aboriginal women. Despicable attitudes of predatory sexual behaviour were then depressingly common, with up to 90% of all racially based murders reportedly occurring, after white settlers kidnapped indigenous women.

The overall cultural shock of confronting life in the outback on a daily basis was almost overwhelming for Evie Maunsell, and indeed most of the early settlers. 21-year-old Evie left a

Indigenous men spear fishing in river

comfortable English home to come to Australia as a companion to a rich woman friend. Within weeks she married Charles Maunsell, who she first met after arriving in Sydney.

Soon after she travelled 400 kilometres from Cairns, by buckboard and buggy to the disease infected Cape York Peninsula. The tropical climate produced what other settlers described as "nine months of summer and three months of hell". On regular occasions the young English woman, from a background of genteel and gracious living, was confronted by poisonous snakes and spiders, dangerous floods and life threatening encounters with hostile natives

> *"Dusty patch in isolation, bare slab walls and earthen floor.*
> *And a blinding drought blazing from horizon to the door."*
> *("The Last Review", Henry Lawson)*

At least Evie Maunsell had a bed to hide under when danger threatened. Other pioneer families would have considered owning a bed to be the ultimate in luxury. Many often slept on chaff bags stuffed with grass.

Their first homes were often tents or tarpaulin structures attached to the dray in which they first travelled to their outback destination. Some families then graduated to bark huts and humpies, or even slab huts if timber was available. Wattle and daub huts were also prevalent. They had the advantage of staying relatively cool in summer and warm in winter, but they also often harboured scorpions and centipedes. The first settlers automatically shook their boots to start the day, and unwelcome night visitors would sometimes tumble out onto the earthen floor.

Newspapers were frequently used as wallpaper to keep out chilly or hot winds, while goat, possum or kangaroo skins were favoured as floor mats. Some German settlers in South Australia built stone houses, while their counterparts in Queensland favoured timber huts raised on stilts.

Mrs J. Foote, a pioneer woman from the NSW western plains, described the furniture her family used in 1878.

> "...the furniture was not of a description to require much workmanship; a table roughly made of red gum...(while) our wagon seats with cushions made comfortable sofas, and the earth floor was covered in bags...Two logs hollowed out served as washing tubs."

Eighteen year-old Catherine Herbig had the first of her 16 children in the trunk of a huge South Australian red gum tree, which had previously been hollowed out by local aborigines. This hardy pioneer outlived her husband by 40 years, and survived until she was in her 90s. The deprivations suffered by the woman depicted in Henry Lawson's classic short story, "The Drover's Wife", seemed of little consequence compared to the life of this amazing pioneer. Apart from her immediate family, Catherine Herbig did not write or speak to anyone in her native English for most of her life, in the isolated environment where she lived.

Most 19th century pioneer women had large families. During child birth, the mothers were usually attended to by a midwife, who might be an experienced local woman with some nursing experience. Many of these midwives became local legends, because of the long distances they sometimes travelled in the dead of night. One such woman was Miss Kathleen Waterhouse, a district nurse in South Australia's Riverland district during the early 1920s. She regularly travelled to patients in remote areas on a railway maintenance trolley, which was powered by a relative or local worker.

Mary Jane Cobden was another heroine of the outback. After being widowed with ten children in 1896, she became a midwife around Humula in the NSW Riverina. Mrs Cobden became a familiar sight, riding side saddle on her black mare over long distances of around 80 kilometres, and inclement weather or dangerous vagrants didn't deter her. Often she crossed swollen creeks in thunderstorms to deliver babies and between 1900 and 1923 it is estimated that she assisted in at least 90 births.

On one lonely trek she was assaulted by a dangerous young male drifter; after that unpleasant incident Mary Jane Cobden carried a revolver on her missions of mercy. Often this amazing woman would stay on at the homestead assisting with washing and ironing duties, but before she departed from the homestead she made sure her gun was loaded.

Child deaths were common and these tragedies had a profound effect on outback women who were mostly isolated from their own mothers and other family members. Often, if a midwife was not available, the planned burial of a deceased infant would become the mother's responsibility, which added greatly to the trauma of having just lost her baby.

Man sitting outside
a bush humpy,
Australia, c1887

One especially heart rending example was Elizabeth McCallum, who resided on South Australia's Eyre Peninsula. Between 1852 and 1870, Ms McCallum had 11 children, and after her son John died of diphtheria in 1872, she feared she was the carrier of the disease. Consequently she removed and burnt all her clothes and bathed herself in a convenient creek before returning home. However, despite her own immunity, only three of her children survived. Fortunately she later gave birth to two other children, but by then her husband was blind and she had the sole responsibility of managing their farm. Despite such tragedies, the resourceful woman apparently remained cheerful and uncomplaining. After giving birth overnight to one of her brood, Elizabeth cooked breakfast for the family early next day, after proudly announcing that she had "a new bonny wee boy".

The resilience of such people was amazing, but many people like Jessie S. Miller from the Darling Downs in Queensland discovered unexpected rewards in outback life. In April 1910, she reported cheerfully in a letter to an English friend that:

> "Every evening we light big bonfires, four of them, to try and frighten them (mosquitoes), away…I must mention the sunset and stars. The finest are beautiful beyond words to describe…if only I could make you see it, standing along on the plain surrounded by the lone, lone bush."

Dust storms, droughts and bushfires were nightmares in many areas.

An anonymous Victorian defined the seasons he experienced in the following terms.

"With the exception of an occasional spring, we reduce the seasons to three-summer, winter and hell, the time when the bushfires are raging."

Even carrying water for household use presented problems. Various forms of transport, such as kerosene tins, petrol drums, tanks on drays and buckets were used to ferry back-breaking supplies of the precious fluid to houses. Water was never wasted. All family members shared the same contents for a weekly bath, and that same water was then used for the household vegetable garden. Sometimes washing of clothes was done in the creek, before they were dried and returned to the house.

If bore or dam water was available, life was easier. Sometimes storage wells were up to 70 metres deep, and near the NSW town of Tumbarumba one cook reportedly found a frog in the jelly that she had lowered into her well to cool!

In larger and more luxurious homes, wash houses sometimes appeared. They were bricked additions with metal troughs which were heated from underneath by a fire box.

Some house proud women became quite competitive about their domestic skills. In 1917, Kathleen Blackwood, from The Rock near the NSW town of Wagga Wagga, remembered one lady being so keen to be the first in the neighbourhood to hang out her Monday morning washing, that she would rise early and hang dry clothing out on the line!

Where possible, cultivating garden produce was a priority, and much pride was taken with fruit, vegetable and herb gardens. Fruits were often bottled or made into jams, and in times of need stinging nettles and stems and leaves of pumpkins would be included on dinner plates.

Sometimes candles were made from clarified fat or tallow, which was sometimes mixed with beeswax. Lard mixed with alum was also used and kerosene lamps began to appear in outback dwellings after 1850.

Interaction with indigenous people helped add variety to outback meals, and "bush tucker" supplements of fruits, roots, nuts, berries, herbs, wild honey, kangaroos, wombats, bandicoots, kangaroo rats, koalas, swans and goannas appeared on some outback dinner tables from the bush environment.

From around 1850 damper became popular especially on stockmen's camp fires. Flour, salt and water were the three basic ingredients of this outback staple food. The damper was buried in the coals of an open camp fire, before being covered with ashes, and turned until it was cooked. After 1855 camp ovens began to be used, but the smaller and more transportable American ovens soon became more popular. Light timber, Spinifex in desert country and wattle in the high country were used to fuel the ovens.

Outback cooks in droving teams or at bush pubs, were notoriously temperamental and unreliable. They mostly learned their trade by trial and error and had a reputation for quitting their job at a moments notice. "Cooks would growl if a snake bit them," was a laconic description afforded to them by one experienced bushman.

A few were given grudging respect. Jame Brunton Stephens recalled a typical outback cook he knew in the late 1880s, whom he described in the following terms.

"He was lazy, he was cheeky, he was dirty, he was sly.
But he had one virtue, and its name was rabbit pie".

Another "back of beyond" cook received the following dubious eulogy.

"Here lies the body of Watts the guy.
He cooked for ten shearers and nine of them died."

Farm animals provided regular supplies of meat, and one outback resident recalls regularly eating mutton three times a day—chops, cold meat and then a joint for the evening meal. By the late 19th century, wild rabbits often supplemented a family's meat needs.

This animal was first brought to Port Jackson with the "First Fleet", and by 1890 the population of the introduced rodent reached plague proportions over much of the continent. By the late 1890s, carcasses and skins from this national pest earned valuable extra money for needy families, and they also became a secondary source of meat, especially in rural areas.

Once rabbits reached plague proportions, eating them was considered to be unacceptable for socially ambitious families. Consequently those wishing to "keep up appearances", would never admit to including rabbit on their dinner table.

Around the late 1890s Coolgardie safes were used to preserve perishable food for brief periods of time. The invention of the Singer sewing machine proved a godsend to outback

Patsy Durack, manager of Argyle Downs, c1930

Mary Durack and friends at Argyle Downs Station, 1942

women, when a Sydney agency for the product became available in 1865. Wives and older daughters became proficient with sewing their own curtains, children's clothes, underwear and winter garments.

The Duracks were a famous pioneering family, being the first to establish successful cattle stations in the rugged East Kimberly area of Western Australia. In that remote region, the family pioneered the growing of cash crops in the rich alluvial soils of the Ord River Valley. The area later became

Elsey Station

the forerunner for the Ord River Irrigation Scheme.

Back in the 1880s Patsy Durack and his two brothers built the Argyle Downs Homestead, after taking two years to trek from Queensland with wagons, carts and approximately 2,000 head of cattle. Decades later, in 1971, the homestead was dismantled at its original site and reconstructed stone by stone in its new location. This move became necessary because of the danger of floods, once the Ord River was dammed. The old homestead is now a public museum.

Elizabeth Durack with one of her Aboriginal paintings, 1971

The Duracks occupied a property the size of Belgium, after they dispossessed the original indigenous inhabitants. It seems ironic that the property is now operated by local aborigines, many of whom remember their "white fella bosses" with much fondness.

Some family members gained notable fame beyond the boundaries of their vast property. Mary Durack (OBE, OA) became famous as an author, before she died in 1994 at the age of 81. *Kings In Grass Castles* and *Keep Him My Country* were two of her notable best sellers.

Her sister, Elizabeth Durack, illustrated some of Mary's books and became an acclaimed and controversial artist in her own right. Shortly before she died in 2000 at the age of 85, Elizabeth Durack shocked establishment figures in the Australian art world, when she revealed a sensational secret. Not only had this single mother and fierce champion for reconciliation become famous under her own name as an artist: she had also created typically aboriginal type paintings under the pseudonym of Eddie Burrup.

Both sisters were daughters of Michael Patrick Durack, who was a famous Kimberly Ranges pioneer.

Peter Durack, a former Rhodes Scholar and later a Queens Counsellor, enjoyed an outstanding state and federal political career. He served as a Western Australian Senator for 23 years after first being elected to the Commonwealth Upper House in 1971. Senator Durack served both as Minister for Repatriation, and Attorney-General, in Federal Liberal Governments. He wrote several books on legal matters, before he passed away in 2008 at the age of 82.

Elsey Station rivals Argyle Downs with its rich history. This Roper River property was first established in 1880. It is located about 90 kilometres south of the NT town of Katherine, and was the third such station to be established in the Australian outback. The property incorporates approximately 5,000 kilometres of land, which means that Elsey Station is geographically larger than some European countries

It was an arduous trip to Elsey Station for Aeneas and Jeannie Gunn when they first arrived in 1902. The newly married couple first sailed from Melbourne to Port Darwin, before moving onto to Pine Creek by train. The remainder of the long journey was undertaken on horseback. Jeannie Gunn (writing under the name of Mrs Aeneas Gunn) later became a celebrated author, with two of her books (*We of the Never Never* and *The Little Black Princess*) becoming established best sellers. Sadly, her husband Aeneas contacted malarial dysentery, and he died only 12 months after arriving at the homestead.

In February 2000, this vast property was handed back to

local indigenous people by Senator John Herron, the then Federal Minister for aboriginal Affairs. A full time fencing post was established to help boost employment in the area. Today over 130, 000 tourists visit Elsey Station each year.

For young children in many outback homes long distance lessons or home-based education was squeezed in between domestic duties. Verandas or kitchens often became the homestead classroom. On rare occasions governesses or station tutors were available for hire.

Between the 1840s and 1870s bush schools appeared in some areas. Attendance was not compulsory until "free, secular and compulsory education" was introduced into the various states in the late 19th century. Students would walk or ride ponies to the school building, and marching drills and bible readings were important areas of the curriculum. Finding suitable accommodation was difficult for women teachers, and their rates of pay were much lower than their male counterparts.

Soon after the Royal Flying Doctor Service (RFDS) delivered outstanding health benefits to outback Australia, the School of The Air was established. Resources such as

A typical bush school. Yathella, NSW c1900s

Afghans loading a camel train Bourke, NSW, c1912

pedal radios became available for health care in outback homesteads, and in 1946 Miss Adelaide Miethke realised the educational potential of this vast communication network in isolated areas of the continent.

Miss Miethke, then Vice-President of the RFDS and a former inspector in South Australian government schools, noted that most outback children were adept at using the new technology. Consequently she campaigned successfully to have the school lessons transmitted through the two way radio system.

The first lessons were broadcast in 1948 from the RFDS base at Alice Springs, and eight years later School of the Air (SOA) programs had been established in other states. Today Tasmania and the Australian Capital Territory (ACT) are the only areas that don't see the need to provide this service. The SOA curriculum now caters for secondary students, for gifted and remedial pupils and adult education. High frequency (HF) radio transceivers have replaced pedal radios, and computers have become a vital learning tool. Australia is undoubtedly a global pioneer in its provision of educational programs for students in isolated areas.

Radio telephones and wirelesses also helped break down the social isolation of station life, and this communication link became the catalyst for an improved social life for outback dwellers. It became easier to publicise race meetings,

Lifestyles of Pioneer Families

dances, sporting matches, Christmas parties and other special events. Women members of families especially enjoyed "dressing up" for these enjoyable social occasions.

In Central Australia, Afghans (who were more likely to have originated from Pakistan or northern India) and their camel trains usually appeared about twice a year, carrying unusual products from city markets. They would collect goods for sale from the last rail head at Oodnadatta and transport them up into the interior as far north as Alice Springs.

Between 1860 and the 1920s, the Afghan camel trains provided a commercial and social link with pioneer families, until they were superseded by the expanding railway system. Roddah Singh from Maree was a familiar Afghan trader of that era. However, once hawkers of his ilk vanished from the outback, their abandoned camels became feral, and they, along with wild pigs and goats, still represent a threat to pastoral land in the Northern Territory.

As a boy, Bernard O'Reilly from Queensland's Lamington Ranges, nostalgically recalled sporadic but exciting visits from Jundah Singh, who would "come with his van full of secret sliding panels and drawers containing goods...comparable with the riches and mysteries of Jundah's native India".

People from isolated areas would indulge themselves in shopping sprees, eagerly purchasing unusual items such as calico, gingham, clay pipes, pots and pans, hurricane lamps, socks, beads, glassware, sardines, building materials and farm equipment.

On larger properties, emigrant English women from the "servant class" would provide often unreliable domestic help, while wards of the state or aboriginal women also undertook this role. Older daughters of pioneer families were entrusted with the care of younger siblings and they sometimes worked as servants in neighbouring stations.

Dorothy Maguire recorded her 1860s to 1870s childhood experiences in Kangaroo Valley, on the NSW South Coast.

"We had no clock, having to guess the time by seeing the tree shadows turn around for 12 o'clock, or hear the hourly laugh of the jackass (kookaburra) that we called 'the settler's clock'.

We worked 44 hours a week. In early days we lived on damper. Later we bought a camp oven.

When crops were ripening, it was my job, wet or dry, to keep the birds off the crops, by running up and down to frighten them."

The pioneers led uniquely challenging lives. Nancy Howard's great grandmother was a pioneer woman who helped run an isolated property near Mudgee in NSW. Nancy honoured her in her tribute poem, "The Pioneer"

"Long ago in a rough slab house,
Dwelt a woman of noble heart.
She toiled each day to rear her sons,
And helped her man on the cattle run.
She rode side-saddle with babe on her knee
Chasing scrub cattle in the wild country."

Only basic and primitive accommodation could be expected in outback hotels. A communal shower, which sometimes produced hot water from an artesian bore, was situated at the end of a corridor or on the back veranda. The toilet hole was usually located near a woodheap, and any billiard table on the premises resembled a relief contour map. One hotel near Sharks Bay in the far north-west of Western Australia (then dubbed "the land of sin, sorrow and sand") was regularly flooded by sea water during the cyclone season.

Bedding was usually a mattress on the floor and meals were sustaining but entirely predictable. Beef or mutton was served three times a day, along with potatoes, pumpkin, tinned fruit, rice and tapioca. Helpings were usually plentiful and the cost minimal.

Respectful rituals usually accompanied outback funerals. Drinkers at any local hotel would leave their beers untouched on the bar and stand bareheaded outside the premises when a funeral hearse passed. Horses usually pulled outback people through life and the same applied in death. One could expect to see massive black horses pulling the hearse and black ostrich feathers were sometimes displayed in the corners of the vehicle. The undertaker tended to be a flamboyant character, who might wear a black silk hat. He would theatrically raise a black gloved hand to indicate a change in direction and occasionally he'd tie black crepe paper streamers to the side of the horse drawn hearse.

Sport has always been a popular point of social contact in the outback. The Todd Regatta in Alice Springs, where competitors run rather than row along a dry creek bed in outrageously designed "boats", is still an annual highlight for both locals and visitors. Every year the outback hamlet of Birdsville in Queensland is swamped with tourists making their annual pilgrimage to watch their favourite horses and jockeys compete in the Birdsville Cup. Many southern state residents also escape cold winter days to attend the popular Darwin Cup, which is usually held in pleasantly warm weather conditions at the "top end". Outback cricket matches are a source of fun and boisterous mischief too.

The late Peter Young became involved with the Wave Hill

The Wave Hill Cricket Club

Cricket Club when he was stationed nearby with the Northern Territory Police Force. Wave Hill is a small settlement on the WA and NT border, not far from the township of Halls Creek. Ringers, camp cooks, mechanics and others travel many kilometres to play in a Wave Hill cricket match. The event can last for as long as a week when associated social activities are pencilled into the program. Transport to the venue is usually by four-wheel drive, bed and breakfast facilities are the players' own swag and tucker box and visitors sleep out in the open at the "starlight motel".

The centre of culture and entertainment at Wave Hill, is Frank's Bar and Grill, the popular name for the licensed premises that adjoins the cricket ground.

Peter Young retained fond memories of happy days at Wave Hill. Before cancer claimed his life, he wrote the following poem, which captures the companionship, humour and enthusiasm that are characteristic features of many sporting events in outback Australia.

Lifestyles of Pioneer Families

*"You may tread the hallowed precincts
Of The Oval or at Lords,
You may see a Test in Sydney,
Or join Melbourne's teeming hordes.
But you've never seen a cricket match,
I fear you never will,
'Til you've seen the boys in action
On a clay pan at Wave Hill.*

*Now Brisbane has the Gabba,
And Sydney had its hill,
But the place that they all envy
Is Frank's famous Bar and Grill.
You may speak about Don Bradman,
O'Reilly and Clem Hill,
But their exploits tend to pallor
With the mention of Wave Hill.*

*They'll collect for causes worthy,
Or a mate that's down and 'flat',
And they'll gather up the proceeds
In Buck's old battered hat.
But when they've bowled the final over,
Or bad light has stopped play,
To Frank's Bar and Grill inviting
They wend their weary way.*

*Where the atmosphere is friendly,
Abounding with good cheer,
And they quaff the gallons lustily,
Of cold and welcome beer.*

*But the memories I will cherish,
I know I always will,
Are of hours playing cricket
On a clay pan at Wave Hill."*

CHAPTER THREE:

MEMORABLE OUTBACK CHARACTERS

Hard drinking still resonates with the image of some outback residents and in bygone years shearers were especially notorious for their huge consumption of alcohol.

Rumours about binge drinking bouts after sheep-yard contracts ended, were often accurate. Many shearers and rouseabouts in outback areas were known to indulge in "booze benders" for several days, and the drunken episodes would only end when all their hard earned money ran out.

One drinking spree on a remote area of the Western Australian coast had an unexpected outcome for a member of the group. After one lapsed into a drunken stupor, his thoughtful mates loaded him onto a boat departing from Australia—he was very surprised when he woke up in Singapore harbour! He felt a little happier when all his drinking mates were there

Two swagmen resting beneath a tree, c1887

to greet him when the ship returned to Australia.

Swagmen were familiar characters on tracks further out. They would unexpectedly appear at homesteads seeking food in exchange for odd jobs, with their well rolled swags wrapped in canvas on their back, a tucker bag hanging over their left shoulder, a blackened billy can in their right hand and bowy-angs below their knees. Pioneer women would tend to have a gun close at hand, if any swagmen dropped by when their husbands were away. Sometimes Indian or Syrian hawkers, in their covered horse-drawn wagons, would also appear from nowhere, as well as gaily painted and ornately carved gypsy caravans.

Stock horses were an invaluable asset for the early settlers. Reliable teams of horses would carry heavy loads all day, existing often on polluted water, salt bush and dried grass, before being hobbled at night.

The stockmen who guided the teams (those often legendary Australian drovers) were an essential part of outback life; no station could have survived without them. The drovers stocked the cattle and sheep runs and guided fattened livestock to markets. Even today, nearly every barbecue lover has a stockman to thank for the red meat that is thrown on the barbie.

THE GREAT LEAP

Blue Lake, in the South Australian town of Mt Gambier, is the site of two now legendary achievements by Australian horsemen.

It has been a popular tourist spot since Europeans first arrived in the area. During the colonial era a fence was erected to protect the public from falling approximately 70 metres off a narrow ledge onto sharp rocks near the lake below.

In 1864 a newly married local guest house owner, accepted a wager to jump a horse over the Blue Lake fence and onto a ledge high above the sharp drop. The reckless dare devil horseman was Adam Lindsay Gordon the famous poet, jockey and politician.

During the early 1850s, a 20-year-old Gordon arrived in Adelaide from London. He gained employment as a South Australian mounted policeman and in 1853 Gordon was stationed in the towns of Mt Gambier and Penola. Two years later he became a horse breaker and he also gained fame as a steeplechase jockey. Gordon suffered serious falls throughout his acclaimed racing career and head injuries from some of these accidents, may explain the frequent bouts of depression that plagued his later life.

Despite such mishaps, there was no doubting his horse riding prowess. At one Melbourne Hunt Club Steeplechase meeting, Adam Lindsay Gordon rode three winners in the one day. His

Adam Lindsay Gordon

most enduring and daring feat, however, was the famous Blue Lake leap at Mt Gambier in 1864.

Hundreds of excited onlookers watched Gordon guide his mount, "Red Lancer", safely over the fence. It was rumoured that Lindsay turned his horse at right angles in mid air to facilitate a safe landing and cheers broke out when both horse and man landed safely on the ledge.

Soon after, the local hero was elected to the South Australian Upper House, but the restless Gordon tired of political life within two years. By then he was writing some fine narrative poetry, but financial success continued to elude him. The often impoverished poet moved first to Ballarat and then to Melbourne, where he became friendly with key figures in the literary world, such as Marcus Clarke and Henry Kendall. However in 1870, shortly after he realised that he could not afford to have a poetry anthology published, the 37-year-old Adam Lindsay Gordon shot himself dead near the suburb of Brighton.

Poems such as "The Sick Stockman" received much acclaim, and Gordon remains the only Australian poet to have a bust statue displayed in London's Westminster Abbey. There is also a statue of Gordon outside Parliament House in Spring Street Melbourne, on which is inscribed the following well-known stanza from one of his poems.

> *"Life is mostly froth and bubble,*
> *Two things stand like stone—*
> *Kindness in another's trouble,*
> *Courage in your own."*

Unfortunately, the troubled poet succumbed to his own troubles, but many admire his achievements. Every year the "Froth and Bubble Festival" takes place near the impressive Spring Street statue and the poetical works of Adam Lindsay Gordon are still honoured by modern loyal supporters.

THE OUTBACK HORSE WHISPERER

Thirty-two years after "Lindsay's leap" at Mt Gambier, the same feat was emulated by a then 26-year-old Lance Skuthorpe, a charismatic character who provided memorable entertainment for outback families over many decades.

Lance Skuthorpe

After accepting the dare to survive a jump over the Blue Lake fence in 1896, Skuthorpe inspected several horses as candidates, before he finally chose a seven-year-old jumper and former steeplechase performer, owned by a local farmer named Boyce. Skuthorpe subjected his mount, "Wallace", to short but intensive training sessions, before making the bold attempt. The jump was executed safely, but Wallace reportedly staggered slightly, before quickly steadying, after landing on the narrow ledge. When the triumphant Skuthorpe collected his winnings, Boyce allowed him to keep the horse.

Lance Skuthorpe was born at Hilltop near Kurrajong in outback NSW, but soon after the family moved to the Moree district, in the north-western corner of the state. His father Jim was a bad-tempered bully and when Skuthorpe was only seven-years-old, his mother allowed the young boy to live off the land for some time with Jack Dick Skuthorpe, his flamboyant uncle.

A dinner jacket and tomahawk were two

items that Jack Dick usually included in his swag, and this lovable man introduced his nephew to the lifestyle of the Australian bush. By the time the youngster returned to his family home, his comprehensive outdoor experiences had produced an accomplished bushman.

Before long his show business talents became obvious and Skuthorpe and Wallace became familiar figures in rural communities. The noted storyteller and rough-rider introduced himself as "Professor" LA Skuthorpe to elevate his status with audiences. He also informed crowds that he was related to Charles Dickens through his mother, whose maiden name had been Dickens. Skuthorpe often began a tour with Australian poetry recitations, but it was his peerless performances as a horse tamer that won him fame.

Skuthorpe gently and patiently used tree branches and his soft fingers to calm the wildest of horses, and his skills became legendary. At Hawkesdale in Victoria, he reportedly rode seven different and previously unridden horses in a little over seven minutes. Furthermore, his first fall off a bucking horse allegedly did not occur until he was over 80-years-old. Only Skuthorpe could tame the notorious out law horse, "Bobs", who reputedly tossed off around 800 other riders before the Professor proved to be his master. Bobs and Skuthorpe once presented a special performance for the NSW Governor, Sir Henry Rawson. Another favourite outlaw horse of Skuthorpe's was "Snips", who often had its four feet off the ground when it bucked off numerous other riders.

Celebrity friends of the famous horse tamer included Sir Sidney Kidman and Banjo Paterson. Skuthorpe also produced a special performance of his riding skills for the Duke of York (who later became King George VI of England). The Royal guest had travelled to Melbourne in 1901, to launch the

Commonwealth's first Parliamentary sitting.

The master rough-rider, showman, fighter, athlete, naturalist, punter and raconteur seldom hung onto the vast amounts of money he regularly earned, and debt collectors were frequently on his trail. He had three children from his second marriage to Violet King and both his son, Lance junior, and daughter Violet, became accomplished horse riding performers.

Lance Skuthorpe senior was deaf from around the age of 40, but the outback legend lived an active life until cancer claimed him in 1958. His son, Lance junior, declared after his father passed away, that "in Heaven the horses are whinnying" and the many who admired this warm, fun loving character, agreed with these sentiments.

It was once said of this extraordinary man that, "if Lance Skuthorpe had been born a few centuries earlier, he would have sailed down the Spanish Main with a cutlass between his teeth". In many ways he was a modern swashbuckling adventurer.

In 1900 he rode buck jumpers in the lions' den under the big top at Wirth's Circus and in 1911 an audience of over 100,000 flocked to see his much publicised exhibition at the Sydney Showgrounds. The venue could not cope with such large numbers, so Skuthorpe attempted to refund the public their admittance money, after organisers were forced to cancel the performance. The multi-skilled Lance Skuthorpe senior was also an accomplished bare knuckle fighter and so fleet of foot, that he finished third in the 1894 Stawell Gift.

THE MAN FROM SNOWY RIVER

*"He sent the flint stones flying,
but the pony kept his feet,
He cleared the fallen timber in his stride.
But the man from Snowy River
never shifted in his seat—
It was grand to see that mountain
horseman ride."
("The Man from Snowy River",
A.B. "Banjo" Paterson)*

Above: Andrew Barton "Banjo" Paterson
Below: The grave of Jack Riley

Jack Riley was a significant outback legend. However, Riley would not have achieved long-lasting recognition for his horsemanship, if the famous Australian poet, Andrew Barton "Banjo" Paterson, had not immortalised him in his epic poem "The Man from Snowy River".

But was Jack Riley the sole inspiration behind Paterson's narrative masterpiece? Paterson himself appeared to reject this notion, in conversations with others, after the poem achieved fame.

In 1936 (nearly 50 years after the poem was published) Banjo Paterson disclosed to Tom Mitchell, a leading member of a famous Upper Murray family, that the man from Snowy River was largely an imaginary person. In previous yarns about the origin of the daring rider, the celebrated author and poet admitted that his creation was partly based on Jack Riley's exploits, but that the deeds of other noted riders also influenced the description of the death-defying mountain ride. Other renowned horseman of that era, including Wright from Delegate, Jim Spencer from Jindabyne, and Charlie McKechnie from Adaminaby, could have influenced the personae of Patterson's fictional hero.

Annie Bryce, a member of a resolute pioneering family that took over an isolated property called Wonnangatta Station in north-eastern Victoria during the late 19th century, added her own list of acclaimed horseman, in a long narrative poem entitled "Some Gippsland Riders". Bryce inferred that Harry Smith from Eaglevale, Dargo Norton, wild Bob Goldie, Will Lee, Tom Phelan and a rider named Cullane, would all have rivalled the imaginary deeds of either "The Man From Snowy River" or "Clancy of the Overflow". Around Corryong, however, where he lived much of his life, most residents are still adamant that it was Jack Riley who was the real "Man from Snowy River".

Riley was reportedly aged 13 when he arrived in Sydney from Ireland in the early 1850s. He joined other optimists in the Omeo gold rush, before working with his sister as a tailor. After she married, Riley became a stockman near the Upper Murray town of Corryong, where he became a legendary horseman.

Before long this reticent and very private man, settled in a bush hut on flat land in Tom Groggin at the foot of Mt Kosciusko Australia's highest peak. He was placed in charge of this important solitary cattle run and the grey-whiskered man virtually lived as a hermit in this challenging and remote location.

He had the reputation of being a cantankerous man, who only tolerated company when visitors plied him with whiskey. In his younger days, it was alleged that Riley had been wrongfully accused of cattle duffing, for which he was imprisoned for six months. If this rumour is true, it would partly explain why Riley distrusted and shunned mainstream society.

The lone horseman seems to have been a magnet for celebrity literatures figures. In 1911 Riley became so gravely ill that a Catholic priest, who was stationed over 100 kilometres away in Albury, drove up to Riley's mountain shack to deliver the last rites. The man of God was Father Patrick Hartigan who, under the pseudonym of "John O'Brien", wrote an anthology of poems titled *Around the Boree Log and other Verses*. The classic Australian poem "Said Hanrahan" was one of the poems include in this highly acclaimed anthology. Father Hartigan's visit must have been beneficial for Riley survived another three years. He eventually passed away at the age of 73, while being stretchered out of his rugged habitat to the nearest hospital.

Today Jack Riley's influence dominates the district where he still remains famous. The inscription on his headstone at the Corryong cemetery reads, "In Memory of The Man From Snowy River, Jack Riley Buried here 16th July 1914". Every autumn the Man From Snowy River Festival, is staged in the town.

> *"And down by Kosciusko, where the pine-clad ridges*
> *raise their battlements on high,*
> *Where the air is clear as crystal,*
> *and the white stars fairly blaze*
> *At midnight in the cold and frosty sky...*
> *The man from Snowy River is a household word today,*
> *And the stockmen tell the story of his ride."*
> *("The Man from Snowy River", A.B. "Banjo" Paterson)*

WALTZING MATILDA

The swagman (a villain who stole sheep from a squatter before committing suicide) depicted in Paterson's lyrics for "Waltzing Matilda", may also have been based on a real life outback character.

In 1894 tensions between union and non-union labour in the shearing industry reached boiling point, and, following a shoot-out at Dagwood in outback Queensland, a woolshed was burnt to the ground. Miraculously, no one was killed in the violent confrontation, but 25-30 kilometres away the shot body of Samuel "Frenchy" Hoffmeister was discovered.

Hoffmeister, a prominent unionist, was described as being a Bavarian anarchist and "a bit mad". There was much debate about the circumstances surrounding his death, with some believing his fatal wounds had occurred during the woolshed gun fight. Consequently, when suicide was listed as being the official cause of death, many observers were sceptical.

In relation to the song's lyrics, it may also be relevant that, at the time of the siege, a butchered sheep was found in the area, and that a "waltzing matilda" (local expression for a swagman) had been sighted nearby.

Around the time of the woolshed siege, Banjo Paterson went to Winton to woo a woman named Sarah Riley, who was a guest at Dagworth cattle station. According to legend, Paterson wrote the lyrics for "Waltzing Matilda" while his hostess at Dagworth, Christina MacPherson, was playing a tune on the piano.

Within weeks the composition was widely sung throughout the district. Today it is very much a national song, which has been sung with much gusto on World War battlefields. It is also regularly performed at international sporting contests, when Australians are participating.

Occasionally on outback tracks, one would see a team of as many as 18 bullocks carting heavy loads. The often profane driver or bullocky would urge his team on with a long greenhide whip. The three inch horns of the bullocks appeared dangerous, but most of these powerful beasts were docile animals.

Rabbit and dingo trappers occupy a place in outback culture, and few have a more enduring popularity than Bert Boulton. He came from humble beginnings, and once reportedly commented that, "When I was three-years-old, I wanted to be a horse, because horses had shoes, and I didn't".

During his early adult years, Bert Boulton earned a living as a dingo and rabbit trapper with the Western Australian government, when the famous Rabbit Proof Fence was being erected. In later years, while learning traditional indigenous methods of hunting and gathering, he came across some breathtaking examples of ancient aboriginal art in caves around the Kimberly Ranges.

Bert Boulton shared his love of the outback by hosting tours into different parts of the interior, and his growing fame resulted in his portrait being painted by Rolf Harris, the famous Australian entertainer and artist.

UNSUITABLE FOR PUBLIC RECOGNITION?

John Wilson, a convict transported to Sydney from England for allegedly stealing nine yards of velvet cloth, became a well-known character in the early days of the first settlement. Soon after arriving, Wilson "went bush" and became literate in the local aboriginal dialect while living with indigenous people around the Hawkesbury River area.

Wilson became an excellent bushman and naturalist, who was given the title of "Bun-bo-ee" by his native companions. He immersed himself in their culture, often dressed in kangaroo skins and decorated his body with tribal markings. When he led a party of 16 on a local expedition, Wilson reportedly shot a lyre bird, he also provided accurate information about koalas that were spotted in the wild. It was John Wilson who was credited with the discovery of useful grazing land between Sydney and Goulburn.

During his widespread treks through rugged bush terrain, Wilson may have become the first European to find a way across the previously impenetrable Blue Mountains. It appears he did reach the granite country that characterises the Upper Cox River Valley near Hartley, and this route later proved to be the easiest way across the mountain ranges.

However, irrespective of the merits of Wilson's case, there was little chance of colonial authorities allowing a convict to take credit for such a landmark achievement. It was far more acceptable (and possibly correct) that the respectable trio of William Lawson, Gregory Blaxland and William Wentworth, receive public recognition for the historic achievement.

Wilson returned to the wild in 1799 and in the following year he was killed by an angry indigenous man after allegedly attempting to abduct a young female member of his tribe.

Outback Stories

THE WILD WHITE MAN

John Wilson's counterpart in Port Phillip (which later became Victoria) was a huge 200 centimetre giant of man named William Buckley, who was transported to Port Phillip from England, after allegedly receiving stolen supplies of cloth. Buckley and five other convicts escaped from custody and tried making their way north to the original settlement at Port Jackson.

Before long Buckley was alone and his companions were either apprehended or had surrendered to authorities. The fugitive existed on raw cockles and mussels, as he made his way west along the southern beaches and soon reached Corio Bay, near a small mountain range known as the You Yangs. Buckley continued to journey solo where no white man had ever been; he finally traversed much of what has since become the Great Ocean Road.

Near the entrance of Port Phillip Bay, Buckley was befriended by local indigenous people and he soon embraced their life style. He dressed in animal skins, learned their language and became skilled in their traditional hunting and fishing methods. His aboriginal companions revered him, believing that this huge white man was a spirit person of great importance. As the decades passed, Buckley virtually lost the ability to converse in English while in his new environment on the Bellarine Peninsula. Today, close to the resort town of

Above:
William Buckley
Bellow: William Buckley's Cave

Point Lonsdale, tourists still visit Buckley's Cave, where the escaped felon allegedly lived for some time.

Thirty-two long years after leaving European society, William Buckley met up with three white men at Indented Head near the entrance to Port Phillip Bay. The surprised trio were part of an exploration group being led by John Batman, and the escaped convict was probably apprehensive about how he would be received.

However, the then 55-year-old escapee who at first struggled to communicate in English with his own countrymen, soon became a celebrity. Colonists called Buckley "the wild white man" and his experience of living for over three decades in the local environment was put to good use. William Buckley acted as a link between the new settlers and the local indigenous people. He was made a free man, received rations and the sum of fifty pounds, for acting as an interpreter. Buckley also organised dispersal of gifts to the aboriginal people and the brick laying skills of his youth were utilised in the building of John Batman's house.

In 1837 Buckley resigned from his employment positions in Port Phillip and settled in Hobart where he married a widow who had one daughter. In Van Diemen's Land (later named Tasmania) Buckley became an assistant store keeper and in 1856 he died in a road accident after being thrown out of a gig.

THE OUTRAGEOUS EXPLOITS OF "CAPTAIN STARLIGHT"

Henry Arthur "Harry" Redford

Henry Arthur "Harry" Redford achieved both acclaim and notoriety, after he established a stock route through some of Australia's most barren country.

It occurred after he guided a stolen herd of one thousand prime head of cattle across hundreds of kilometres, from the remote Queensland property of Bowen Downs to livestock markets near Adelaide. The remarkable journey took Redford and his criminal associates through the arid Channel country and Strzelecki Desert in South Australia (now known to be the driest state on the driest continent on Earth) to just near the Great Australian Bight.

It was in 1870 (a decade after Burke and Wills perished in similar country) that Harry Redford instigated his brazen theft. During the journey, he sold a white bull at Artacoona Native Well near Hill Station and he later sold more livestock at Blanchewater Station to the east of Maree. After workers at Bowen Downs discovered the theft weeks after it occurred, a party of stockmen and trackers found the missing white bull when they set off in pursuit.

Initially Redford found safe haven in NSW. He married Elizabeth Jane Scuthorpe at Mudgee in 1871 and the marriage produced at least one child. However, the long arm of the law caught up with the now notorious cattle duffer and in 1872 Harry Redford was arrested in Sydney. He was then extradited to Roma in west Queensland, where he faced trial.

It was a sensational court case. Despite strong evidence to the contrary, the jury found Harry Redford not guilty of cattle theft and the presiding judge could not hide his disbelief.

"Thank God gentlemen, that the verdict is yours and not mine," he declared, after the controversial decision was announced. The Queensland government shared the judge's dismay, as Roma Court was shut down for eight months after Redford walked free.

In his much acclaimed book *Robbery Under Arms*, author "Rolf Bolderwood" (the pen name of Thomas Alexander Browne) partly based his popular bushranger character of Captain Starlight on the exploits of Harry Redford. Consequently, to some of the general public, the notorious cattle duffer became regarded as a gentlemanly rogue.

It is thought that Redford later relocated to the Northern Territory, where it is believed he drowned while attempting to cross a flooded creek in 1904.

THE OUTBACK HUMAN HEADLINE

One could always expect the unexpected from Bill Harney, who was an especially flamboyant outback character.

He was born in the Queensland town of Charters Towers in 1895 and his boyhood years were far from conventional. Harney's formal education ended in primary school and he then became a printer's devil with the Cairns *Morning Post*. His father and he fossicked for gold around Charters Towers and by the age of 12, Bill Harney was droving stock on his own over outback Queensland cattle routes. At the age of 20, he enlisted in the Australian Infantry Force (AIF) and served on the Western Front during World War I hostilities.

After returning to Australia in 1919, Harney drove cattle and delivered mail in the Northern Territory, until he enjoyed a huge windfall in 1921, when the horse he backed heavily, won the Melbourne Cup. The battling outback wanderer won the princely sum of eight hundred and fifty pounds (over $3,000) and with the proceeds he became joint owner of a struggling property named Seven Creeks Lagoon.

Bill Harney then fell on hard times. In 1923 he was gaoled for three months after being charged with horse stealing. Harney allegedly read many classics of English literature, while serving his sentence in Borroloola Prison, before

Bill Harney writing in his journal, Darwin Camp, c1940s

being freed on appeal. After being released, the unpredictable adventurer bought a sailing vessel named "Iolanthe", with money granted to him from a war gratuity. He used his yacht to catch trepang and gather salt in the Gulf of Carpentaria.

On 5th April 1927, 32-year-old Bill Harney married a 17-year-old part aboriginal woman named Linda Beattie, at the Grote Eylandt Anglican Mission Church. The couple produced two children, but the marriage was tragically short-lived, with Linda dying from tuberculosis in 1932. Harney's personal traumas continued, with his daughter Beattie also succumbing to tuberculosis in 1934, and his son Billy perishing 14 years later after a failed attempt to rescue a drowning person.

Between 1940 and 1947, Harney expanded his expertise about aboriginal cultures and traditions, when he worked as a patrol officer and protector of indigenous groups. In 1941 the versatile bushman commenced a writing career and over the next 50 years eight of his very popular bush humour and cook books were published. In 1958 Harney was also involved in successful television and radio programs in Britain, when he shared his war time experiences with J.J.M. Thompson to a large, appreciative audience.

His fascinating diversity of roles continued. During his nomadic lifestyle, Harney worked as a grader driver's assistant in the NT, became an adviser on National Geographic assignments, was appointed as an Uluru park ranger and in 1955 he assisted with the production of the film *Jedda*.

The short, stocky, gregarious and charismatic man remained a consummate raconteur for the remainder of his days. Bill Harney died at his "Shady Tree" home in Mooloolaba, Queensland, on New Years Eve in 1962.

TED'S TALL TALES AND TRUE

Ted Egan singing with a beer carton instrument, Kiama Folk Festival, NSW c1995

Ted Egan remains a bush icon, who has achieved fame as a singer, author, raconteur, media presenter and administrator.

Egan was born in the Melbourne suburb of Coburg and departed for the NT at the age of 16, in search of work and adventure. He was first employed by the Department of Aboriginal Affairs but also worked as a stockman, crocodile hunter, patrol officer, aboriginal reserve superintendent and teacher, before being included in the inaugural National Reconciliation Council.

Ted Egan began recording songs about outback life in 1969 and has released about 30 albums, which often focus on aboriginal traditions and beliefs. He is a gregarious and instinctive entertainer, who sometimes uses only his hands and fingers on an empty beer carton, to provide back up rhythm for his presentations.

As a television presenter, Egan narrated many episodes of *This Land Australia*, which featured many iconic Australian people and locations. He has also co-hosted the popular television program *The Great Outdoors*.

Ted Egan is listed among Australia's National Living Treasures by the National Trust of Australia. In 1993 he received an AM for services to aboriginal people and for being "an ongoing contributor to the literary heritage of Australia through song and verse".

The seemingly ageless man was 71 when he accepted an appointment as Chief Administrator of the NT and this 2003 appointment has since been extended twice. A further honour was bestowed in 2004, when Ted Egan was named as an Officer in the General Division of the Order of Australia.

CHAPTER FOUR:

HEROES OF THE OUTBACK

THE FIRST OVERLANDERS

Soon after Adelaide was first settled in 1826, nearby arable land was either bartered for or seised by the first arrivals. Consequently, overlanders began droving sheep and cattle to newly emerging settlements across the continent, and an Englishman named Joseph Hawdon was one of the first overlanders to take up the challenge.

For nearly a month in 1836, Hawdon drove around 300 sheep from just south of Sydney to the port of Melbourne. He discovered much valuable grazing land near his final destination. The profits gained by the first settlers of that area resulted in Hawdon being rewarded with a fertile grazing property near Westernport Bay.

The then 24-year-old was certainly an enterprising young man. Joseph Hawdon effectively became Melbourne's first postie, operating a 14-day mail service between Melbourne and Yass. The journey covered approximately 650 kilometres, and around half of this territory was occupied by hostile indigenous people. Hawdon then embarked on an ambitious droving trip that transversed much of south-eastern Australia.

On 4th January 1838, Hawdon's party departed from Melbourne and reached Howlong near the Murray River. There, Hawdon collected some cattle from his brother's property and on that leg of the journey he met Charles Bonney, another squatter who joined the Adelaide bound expedition. The two young men formed an efficient leadership group, as Bonney's diplomatic skills with local indigenous people complemented Hawdon's more abrasive personality.

The pair divided the stock, and on 17th January Hawdon met up with Bonney and his flock of over 1,200 sheep at a Goulburn River site. They rested for five days before following Sir Thomas Mitchell's route to the inland rivers. Kangaroos they shot and fish they caught on the journey supplemented their food supplies, but it was a gruelling trip. They experienced very hot weather conditions and fierce electrical storms killed three of their bullocks.

Hawdon and Bonney followed the Goulburn River north until it joined the Murray. The terrain was flat and water supplies were adequate, but some aboriginal groups appeared hostile. The group reached Swan Hill on 11th February, where they established friendly relationships with most of the local indigenous people. They did have to fire a volley of shots over the heads of one threatening group, but Bonney dealt efficiently with the problem and violence was avoided. The aboriginal people of the area were puzzled by the lack of women with the white invaders, and wondered if the heifers in the herd were actually their wives!

At the time the countryside was suffering the effects of a prolonged drought, so crossing the Murray and Darling Rivers presented few problems. As they drew near St Vincent's Gulf sand hills made it difficult for the drays to proceed, and on this leg of the journey Hawdon was nearly accidentally shot by another member of the group.

In the present day Riverland area of South Australia, they discovered a stretch of water that they named Lake Bonney and a friendly local aboriginal named Tenberry guided them further up the Murray. As the river moved to a more southerly position, better grazing lands became evident and on 31st March they sighted St Vincents Gulf, where they met three young white men who were shooting kangaroos.

Governor Hindmarsh provided an enthusiastic welcome on 4th April, after observing the excellent physical condition of most of the herd. Bonney stayed on in South Australia where he later overlanded more arid routes. In 1839 he assisted John Ross, when his exploratory group travelled through the Portland area in south-western Victoria. Hawdon relocated to Victoria where he raised sheep and cattle but he then moved to New Zealand and pursued a political career.

The Joseph Hawdon and Charles Bonney Memorial, Shepparton

John Ross

THE OVERLAND TELEGRAPH ROUTE

In 1870 John Ross was appointed leader of an expedition that preceded the construction of a telegraph line, which would stretch across the entire continent from Adelaide to Darwin. This ambitious project covered 3,200 kilometres of trackless desert, mulga scrub and tropical swamps. John McDouall Stuart was the only previous European explorer to investigate that inhospitable area of Australia, but the potential benefits of success in the operation were enormous. The completion of an overland telegraph system meant Australia could effectively establish communication links with the rest of the world.

This dream became a possibility after the South Australian government ratified an agreement with the British-Australian Telegraph Company. The negotiated completion date for linking Australia from south to north was 1st January 1872, which would then connect with the underwater cable line from Timor. Only 18 months was allocated for completion of the ambitious project. The clock was therefore ticking for administrators such as Charles Todd (the South Australian Postmaster-General and Superintendent of Telegraphs) so that the government could avoid paying overdue penalty rates.

The 53-year-old Ross was an experienced

bushman. In 1830, he had been one of the first of the overlanders, and his support group of Giles, Crisp, Hearne and Harvey also appeared to be well suited to the challenging task.

The expedition's first aim was to find a pass through the eastern McDonnell Ranges. Once this formidable hurdle was overcome, the group would then be able to turn south to meet up with the construction team, which was establishing the connection line from northern Australia. The Ross team had responsibility for obtaining timber for poles and supplying water to workers and their livestock.

Soon after the Ross group began their long inland trek on 8th July 1870, it became obvious that government supplies were inadequate. By August, they experienced more significant problems when they were attempting to take the shortest possible northerly route through the Simpson Desert. Water supplies became perilously scarce and while the explorer's problems were temporary reprieved at the discovery of a creek, local aborigines, whose limited water supplies were being consumed by the European invaders and their livestock, represented an ongoing danger to the group.

The formidable mountain barrier was finally reached, but a way through appeared to be illusionary. Ross and his men searched in vain for ways through the Eastern McDonnell or Fergusson Ranges, before they returned to the creek.

In mid-October the expedition reached the Hugh and Finke Rivers. By then it was obvious that the availability of water supplies would decide the direction of the future overland telegraph route, though Charles Todd still wished to traverse the most direct line through the McDonnell Ranges.

Extremely hot and dry conditions prevailed. The group survived for 36 hours without water, before Ross again uncovered precious supplies. By Christmas of 1870, a way through the ranges remained a mystery, but on New Years Day they came across the tracks that McDouall Stuart's party had left nearly a decade before. The old footprints provided stark evidence about the lack of rain in the dead heart of the continent. They followed Stuart's route to Central Mt Stuart, where fortunately both water and game were plentiful, but other problems began to impact on the group.

The lack of green vegetables in their diet resulted in an outbreak of scurvy, and around that time William Harvey nearly perished after becoming lost. Local indigenous groups again showed their hostility by attempting to trap the explorers in a fire they lit around the group, and other natives tried to steal valuable food supplies.

Criticisms about their lack of progress began to emerge in Adelaide, and Harvey left the expedition. Finally, however, on 11th March 1871, a crucial breakthrough occurred, when G.R. McGinn and W. Whitfield discovered Simpson's Gap to the east of Stuart's original track. New water holes were uncovered, with Stuart (later re-named Alice Springs after Charles Todd's wife) being one of many storage sites scattered along the new route.

Nothing was heard of Ross's party for the whole of April, but finally, on 19th May 1871, the exhausted and ragged explorers reached the southern bank of the Roper River. Better news continued. A more direct route to the north had emerged, which would accelerate the future construction of the line.

Industrial problems briefly surfaced in early June, when workers downed tools in protest about the lack of supplies. However, by then Ross had successfully established the future route that the telegraph line would take and he was much praised for his achievement. Ross himself was too ill from the life endangering trek to make his way back to Adelaide on the overland route. After recuperating in Darwin, he returned to the South

Australian capital by ship.

The original January 1872 deadline for completion of the line was missed, but by 20th June of that year the first messages were transmitted, aided at first by a pony express service. On 22nd August 1872 the line from northern to southern Australia was finally connected, and in October of that year it was linked with the completed underwater link from Timor.

John Ross, South Australia's premier bushman, is still revered for establishing Australia's overland telegraph route.

Planting the first telegraph pole near Palmerston, Darwin, September 1870

Alfred Canning

AN ALMOST IMPOSSIBLE MISSION

On 26th April 1906, Alfred Canning, a 46-year-old Victorian-born surveyor, was appointed by the Western Australian government to lead an expedition that would potentially deliver huge benefits to agriculturalists in the West.

In today's jargon, the proposed venture was almost "mission impossible". Canning was asked to establish a stock route that would link pastoral interests of the East Kimberly area in the far north of WA to markets in the goldfields region of Kalgoorlie and Coolgardie, in the south-east of the vast state. The land, which Canning and his team were asked to survey and service, is one of the most arid areas in the world.

Albert Canning brought impressive credentials to the challenging project. He had previously surveyed approximately 1,800 kilometres of forbidding and isolated country between Esperance and Port Hedland, when the state government financed the installation of a Rabbit Proof Fence. This important project aimed to protect rural properties of the West being ravaged by plagues of rabbits, which had previously devastated much prime land in eastern Australia.

The first new challenge for Canning was to establish a 1,440 kilometre stock route between Wiluna and Halls Creek, in WA's north-west. Once this initiative was completed, tick-prone cattle from the East Kimberly region would be able to by-pass coastal areas where the insect pest thrived, and still arrive in southern livestock sale-yards in good condition.

Loaded with nearly 1500 litres of water and sufficient food supplies, Canning, his second in command Hubert Trotman, seven other associates, 23 camels and two ponies commenced their epic journey towards the end of May. At first, water was plentiful, and the group saved their own precious supplies when they passed near Lake Nuberu and Windich Springs.

By the time the exploration team reached arid areas such as the Little Sandy Desert, they followed an agreed strategy: Canning or Trotman would leave the main group to locate a water supply ahead. The rest of the team would wait at their overnight camp until this vital mission was accomplished. They would then work at improving the water site, hopefully with the voluntary or coerced assistance of local indigenous people. At times, this controversial tactic proved successful; on one occasion a local guide named "Nappa" directed the group to artesian water at Sunday Well, a large source that extended inland for approximately 700 kilometres.

As they pressed on through the Little Sandy Desert, water and stock feed became surprisingly abundant, and under the guidance of another aboriginal dubbed "Bandicoot", they made good progress for the next 300 kilometres. Then another local aboriginal helped the group find water when they entered the Great Sandy Desert, before some Mujingera people showed signs of hostility. On this occasion the team's bellowing camels frightened the menacing natives, so a potential crisis was averted. Canning also shot some cockatoos, which he presented to appreciative locals.

By then the journey had become very difficult. An extensive drought had dried up many soaks and wells in the Great Sandy Desert, and local aboriginal people disappeared as the even drier desert winter closed in. Finally fresh water was discovered at Waddawalla Soak, but by then morale in the group had slumped. Canning needed all his impressive diplomatic skills (and an occasional shot of brandy) to placate disgruntled team members, whose resentments were often further inflamed by Edward Blake, the expedition cook. The number of dried up soaks and wells was increasing, so maintaining positive attitudes became an important priority.

The boring of Lumba Soak fortunately provided plentiful supplies of water, and the countryside gradually became more fertile as the group made its way along Sturt Creek and into the Kimberly Ranges. On 30th October 1906, Canning rode into Halls Creek from Billilura Pool, and telegraphed news of his successful arrival to authorities. He promised to drill further bores on their return trip, so that a well watered and accurately mapped stock route would become available for future drovers. The constant threat of violence escalated on the journey, with a European named Mick Tobin and a disgruntled local aborigine, both being killed in a gun and spear fight. Today Mick Tobin's grave can still be visited on the famous stock route.

The Canning expedition returned to Wiluna 14 months later, after sinking 20 bores and improving nearly 40 aboriginal water holes on their initial journey. Albert Canning received a hero's welcome when he returned to Perth. He agreed to finish establishing the stock route, and Edward Blake was dismissed from his post. The revengeful cook reported to local newspapers that Canning and others had mistreated indigenous Australians during the first expedition. Canning was exonerated by a 1908 Government Commission, after the spiteful allegations were withdrawn. In today's world, it is possible that some actions of Canning and Trotman towards indigenous people, would not be tolerated by authorities.

The return expedition began in April 1908, and on this occasion Canning had the support of 31 men and a year's food supplies. The trip was uneventful until they reached the halfway point of Wiluna. It was there they realised that their food rations would not last, so Canning decided to move ahead of the group to obtain extra supplies. It was planned that he would meet up with the rest of the party at Sturt Creek. Water supplies were also dangerously low when Trotman led the expedition into Halls Creek in November, 1909. By then they had been on outback tracks for over 18 months, but many wells had been either renovated or constructed.

Fortunately extra food arrived two days after their initial supply ran out, and during the time of crisis a laconic Trotman did not attempt to glamorise the desperate situation they faced, when he allegedly made the following blunt statement to his team:

> "It's up to you. We're just about out of tucker, but we've got to finish the wells. We could starve or perish, but apart from that we'll have a good time."

Six of the group elected to remain with the expedition.

Later the team was held up in Wiluna after heavy rain fell, but the local population treated the men like heroes and provided them with generous supplies of food.

Four arduous years after the project first began, Canning was able to provide the following succinct telegram message to the government.

"Work completed. Canning".

His remarkable knowledge of the outback and his superb organising skills, resulted in good water supplies being available in 52 wells along the enormous route, which were no more than 27 kilometres apart.

The stock route was first used in 1909, but problems with local aborigines persisted. In 1911 three Europeans were speared to death at Lake Disappointment, and two others perished in 1922 and 1936 respectively.

Incredibly, in 1929, a then nearly 70-year-old Albert Canning was asked to supervise repairs to some of the wells, a task that took eight months to complete. Rest from his labours only came when he died in Perth at the age of 75.

Alfred Canning and party on the survey trip to mark out the line of the Rabbit Proof Fence, WA c1901

THE MAILMAN WHO ALWAYS DELIVERED

Mail and other supplies have been delivered to isolated dwellings along the remote Birdsville Track (which crosses the state border line between South Australia and Queensland) since the late 1860s, but no other mailman matched the deeds of the legendary Tom Kruze. For over 17 years he regularly delivered letters and parcels each fortnight to outpost dwellings, along one of the loneliest roads in Australia.

Esmond Gerald "Tom" Kruze was born in 1914, he first started driving a mail service vehicle along "the track" for Harry Ding on New Years Day in 1936. Every fortnight, he would confront sand hills, sand drifts, dust storms, flies, bugs and bogs, floods and numerous mechanical break-downs, in his quest to deliver mail to outback people. At times deliveries were understandably late, but Kruze prided himself on letters and parcels finally reaching their destination.

"There will never be a mailman like Tom," was the long standing epitaph from outback clients.

Some of his work experiences, in his trademark 1936 Leyland Badger truck, became legendary. On one of his first trips, Tom was forced to walk in 40°C heat to Mungeranne and then back to Mulka, before he could repair a broken tail shaft.

The Old Birdsville Track, 1963

His round trip, between Marree in South Australia and Birdsville in Queensland, usually lasted seven days, but on one occasion it took six weeks to complete. On another trip, Kruze became bogged at Pandie Pandie and he had to be picked up by helicopter. Pilots often refused to land their planes at water logged stations during the wet season, but Tom Kruze prided himself on overcoming all obstacles in the performance of his duties.

Kruze operated the Birdsville mail contract between 1948 and 1963. His cherished Leyland Badger truck was initially abandoned in the Sturt Stony Desert, but Tom later drove it back to the Birdsville Motor Museum, so that the restored relic could be viewed by the public. His last regular trip along "the track" occurred in 1953 and Tom Kruze then started an earth moving and tank sinking business in the outback.

In 1952 Tom Kruze and his wife Valma starred in a documentary called *Back of Beyond*, which won the Grand Prix award at the 1954 International Film Festival in Venice. Two years later, Tom was the recipient of a Member of the British Empire (MBE) award for "services to the community in the outback…risking his life on many occasions".

Sir William Slim, the then Governor of Australia, made a special flight to Birdsville to present the award to Kruze, but the intrepid postman had been cut off by floodwaters on "the track" and he was unable to attend the ceremony. A year later this mishap was rectified, and Tom Kruze received his MBE decoration in Adelaide.

His family moved to South Australia's capital in 1964, but Tom stayed up north and continued to operate his dam sinking, road building and heavy haulage business. Valma visited him often in his frontier environment and in 2002 the couple celebrated their 60th wedding anniversary.

THE GOLD MEDAL PERFORMANCE

It had to be big—an ultimate "wow" experience. It had to command attention. It had to be perfect.

In show business presentations, first impressions are paramount, as an audience will often pass final judgements on a performance in the first seven seconds. Ultimately, all the predictable and imponderable outcomes gelled in this performance, and the success of the 2000 Sydney Olympic Games Opening Ceremony set the tone for the competition and drew the unreserved applause of a global audience. The "go to" person in the international success story was Steve Jeffrey, a down to earth Australian horse trainer.

Steve Jeffrey grew up in the bushy Sydney suburb of Terrey Hills, where he developed a love of horses by the age of 12. A fine horseman named John Pinnell taught the young boy how to break in horses, a role he soon performed for the famous racehorse trainer Tommy Smith at his Randwick stables. Jeffrey later travelled the racing world in his role, and for three years he was employed as a horse breaker in areas of the USA.

On his return to Australia, Jeffrey worked briefly on a property near Yass, owned by media baron, Rupert Murdoch. He then married and opened up a dry cleaning business. After his marriage ended, the then 38-year-old Jeffrey was lured back into horse breaking by Sandy Langford, a former NSW Mounted Policewoman, with whom Steve Jeffrey later formed a de facto relationship.

In 1998 he was persuaded by a friend to assist him in the recruitment of horse riders, to form part of a tribute to "The Man From Snowy River" segment of the 2000 Olympic Games Opening ceremony. Candidates came from extremely diverse backgrounds. There were old experienced drovers and farmers, as well as children from pony clubs. All participants had to sign a secrecy agreement. Eventually 120 horses and riders were short listed for a choreographed presentation, which would be planned by Jeffrey, Langford and media producer Ignatius Jones.

An effective start to the segment became an essential priority, and Jones asked Jeffrey to find a rearing horse to make an initially dramatic impact on the audience. At first Jeffrey considered this daring concept to be a risky and impractical "pie in the sky" idea, but within a week he mellowed his views. Langford and he finally recommended a strong-willed, easily distracted and obnoxious horse called "Ammo", to be the focal point of the performance.

"Ammo" actually made a promising start, reaching the high success rate of 80% with his huge, spectacular rears at rehearsals, but the novelty soon waned and ten days before the Opening Ceremony, his rehearsal performances became less successful. Around that time Jeffrey was asked to include whip cracking in the routine and the pressure of expectations began to take its toll. Demanding 15-hour work days caused him to lose sleep and drop in weight and he developed a heavy case of flu, only days before the prestigious event began.

Just before the ceremony commenced, "Ammo" became over-excited and even more difficult to handle, but when it counted the magnificent black horse became a star. His second rearing performance in particular was a breath-taking spectacle; the powerful image of horse and rider reflected an image of outback Australia that the world embraced with enthusiasm. As the segment closed, it seemed as if everybody on Earth joined in a spirited rendition of "Waltzing Matilda".

Steve Jeffrey remains a legend. He is still targeted for questions about the 2000 Opening Ceremony, when he conducts horse riding and training exhibitions around the country.

CHAPTER FIVE:

OUTSTANDING WOMEN OF THE OUTBACK

"It was no place for a woman—
where the women worked like men,
From the bush and Jones' Alley come their haunted forms again.
And let this be remembered, when I've answered to the roll,
That I pitied haggard women—wrote for them with all my soul."
("The Last Review", Henry Lawson)

There is no doubt that Gladys Bauer worked as hard as any man. During the 1940s, she was a drover's cook and sometimes she and her four children travelled on outback tracks for up to 20 weeks, when her husband, Henry, was employed as a long distance drover. In 1942 the Bauer family covered three states in one trip, when they accompanied livestock from the NT to Walgett in outback NSW.

Gladys Bauer's routine began around 3am, when she would prepare breakfast for five hungry drovers as well as her family. Stew, curry or mince were the usual choices, and the meals were cooked in a big camp oven. She would then pack up and drive the group's lorry to the next allocated camp. If water supplies were available, Gladys would fill the tank on the way.

Prior to preparing the evening meal she often washed clothes, before hanging them in trees to dry. Fresh bread straight from the oven would be also be available, as the drovers expected meat, brownies and bread each day in their lunches. Her busy day was not over after the evening meal was cooked and the dishes were washed; Gladys, along with the rest of the team, would then have a two hour supervision shift, watching over the herd during the night.

It was always wise to expect the unexpected on such droving trips. One night, after a fierce electrical storm broke out, the herd stampeded and scattered in all directions. A day of travel time was lost while the cattle were retrieved. On another occasion near Mt Isa the team had to cope with a flash flood, after 200ml. of rain fell in a short period of time.

Gladys Bauer's strenuous life was finally rewarded. She finished up owning a new car and her new house was powered by electricity!

> *"A cloud of dust on the long white road,*
> *and the teams go creeping on,*
> *Inch by inch with the weary load;*
> *And by the power of the green-hide goad*
> *The distant goal is won."*
> ("The Teams", Henry Lawson)

Mary Steele became a renowned boss drover around much of Queensland and the NT. This small, reserved woman always dressed primly in Victorian era skirts, but she was as gritty as any of her male counterparts.

During World War II she and her husband, Jack, drove over 1,000 bullocks on long droving treks to markets and little sleep was possible on such gruelling trips.

Around NT stock routes, Elsie Bohning became known as "the petticoat drover". Elsie began mustering, riding and branding at the age of 11, and in later years her husband, children and she managed Helen Springs Station, 160 kilometres north of Tennant Creek. She also found time to portray her lifestyle in verse.

> *"I am travelling down the OT line, and I'm a drover's hand.*
> *I'm making Johnny cakes, and I am handy with a pan.*
> *And I can bend a mob of steers.*
> *Did you hear my stockwhip crack?*
> *No, stockwhips are forbidden, with fat cattle on the track.*
> *Now all you jolly rovers, from hut and camp and town,*
> *Come drink the health of the drover, the king of the overland."*

Various immigrant women brought their own particular customs to outback locations from their countries of origin. By 1851, in the South Australian copper mining towns of Burra and Moonta, about 2,600 Cornish settlers built dugouts for homes; some of these pioneer dwellings still survive today.

In accordance with Cornish traditions, women covered their floors with rag rugs and sewing needs were undertaken in the evenings by candlelight. Cornish pasties were cooked for their husband's lunches in the mines and new babies were delivered at home. Carols by candlelight were a Christmas season highlight and for Yule tide celebrations the churches were decorated with green branches. A singing parade would take place in town and traditional Cornish music was played on flutes, bassoons and other instruments.

From the 1830s, new German immigrants arrived. They were mostly driven from their homeland by religious persecution. At first their new homes in colonial Australia were built from straw and mud. In South Australia, around what is now called the Barossa Valley, German settlers became renowned for their strong work ethic in the orchards and vineyards.

Many German-Australians were shunned in their communities after 1939, when Australia joined allied forces in war against Germany. One of those affected was Ottile Johannsen.

In 1905 Ottile married Gerhardt Andreas Johannsen, a Danish man who soon took out a lease at Deep Well. The couple reached this isolated cattle station, by first catching a train to Oodnadatta, followed by a bone shaking coach ride to their final destination. Gerhardt later constructed a four-room stone house for his wife and three children and he assisted with the births of two of the newly born at the homestead. Ottile, who on one occasion was forced to defend herself from a dangerous attack with a shot gun, spent much time teaching indigenous women how to sew, embroider and crochet.

At the beginning of 1924, Gerhardt Johannsen took over the management of Hermannsburg Mission. There he assisted in the birth of another addition to his family. Ottile became involved in teaching life skills to aboriginal women, as well as supervising her own children's correspondence lessons. Ottile also became a renowned cook, who used many bush foods in her recipes. In the mission gardens she grew date palms that still stand today.

At Hermannsburg the family suffered from the lack of medical facilities. In 1928 it became Ottile's responsibility to nurse her husband through a serious bout of poliomyelitis, but she later needed to be hospitalised in Adelaide after becoming very ill with pleurisy. In later years Ottile Johannsen moved to Alice Springs, where she ran a boarding house and sold the fruits she grew in her own garden. Ottile remained a devout Lutheran, who always observed grace in German before eating meals. She passed away in 1959, at the age of 78.

The procuring of labour to northern Australia locations from South Pacific islands, virtually amounted to slavery. Around the late 1860s many Melanesian people were seduced and even kidnapped from their island habitats, and forced to labour in Queensland sugar cane fields. These "Kanakas", as they were called, usually built thatch homes on stilts, and they became expert market gardeners. Those who later voluntarily chose to remain in Australia, became renowned for their generous hospitality and their coconut palm weaving.

Granny Lum Loy

Chinese immigrants, who were originally attracted to various areas of Australia by the gold rush, also became well known for the bountiful market gardens they established on the fringes of settlements. In the north of the continent, there was frequent intermarriage with aboriginal partners and many of this group became hawkers and cooks. One legendary member of the Chinese-Australian group was a woman known as Granny Lum Loy.

Lum Loy arrived in Darwin by ship in the late 1870s and was adopted by a Chinese storekeeper. Throughout her long life she always wore traditional Chinese clothing and broad-rimmed hats, and, despite her inability to speak English, Lum Loy became a well-known "top end" identity. During her stay near Katherine, Lum Loy's mango orchards contained as many as 200 productive trees and she continued to grow and sell tropical fruits, until she died in 1980 at the age of 93.

THE MOTHER OF THE NORTH-WEST

Emma Withnell somehow survived an extremely traumatic beginning to life in a new country. At the end of a long voyage from England, Emma's ship was blasted by a fierce storm off the north-west coast of Western Australia. Most of the passengers' possessions were swept overboard, but, after the ship ran aground, some items of luggage were deposited by the crashing waves onto an isolated beach. Emma not only lived through the dangerous ordeal; she went on to become a pioneer legend of the West.

Today in Roebourne Western Australia, there is a memorial plaque that describes Emma Withnell as "the mother of the north-west". Her humanitarian work with aboriginal people was revered, but she also became an enterprising entrepreneur in the pearling and mining industries. In total the Withnell family developed 11 pastoral properties in the far north-west of the state. They also overcame significant losses from various cyclones.

Isolation presented many problems for outback women and the plight Elizabeth Tierney faced in 1900 vividly displays the potential dangers that solitary women faced. Mrs Tierney was a widow with six children; she virtually became a hostage in her isolated homestead near the NSW town of Singleton, after a group of aboriginal bushrangers embarked on a murderous rampage. Joe and Jimmy Gardiner, along with Jacky Underwood, had already slaughtered three neighbouring families. Fortunately the violent trio was arrested before the widow and her family were harmed.

LIFE ON THE LINE

Little personal connection with the outside world was available to Atalanta Bradshaw, after her husband Thomas took over the management of a remote overland telegraph station. Supplies from Adelaide only arrived at their homestead once a year and it was impossible to grow green vegetables in the arid conditions. In summer, temperatures sometimes soared to 50% Celsius and flies and mosquitoes were a constant nuisance.

For entertainment, Atalanta, Thomas and their seven children, would ride their horses out into the desert scrub and enjoy a family picnic. Such outings became more accessible after her husband acquired a buggy. Thomas Bradshaw became a skilled photographer during those years and his prints depicting domestic family life became highly valued.

Health care was an unresolved problem in this isolated environment. Atalanta did her best to cater for the needs of local indigenous women, and this unqualified woman also nursed her son, Mortimore, and daughter, Doris, when they became desperately ill with diphtheria and rheumatic fever respectively. Inadequate medical attention also permanently affected Atalanta, as she suffered long term gynaecological problems, after one of her births was assisted by an inexperienced midwife.

In the early years of the 20th century, Atalanta returned to urban life to cater for her children's education. She was 63 when she died in Adelaide in 1929.

TAKE HER AT HER WORD

Some outback women wrote about their experiences off the beaten track, and one who achieved recognition in the literary world was Catherine "Katie" Langloh Parker. As a girl, she was reportedly saved from drowning by a young female aboriginal, which may explain the close affinity she later enjoyed with indigenous people in her adult years.

Katie married at the age of 18 and travelled by train to Bourke in NSW. From there the young bride endured a long and jolting buggy ride over virtually unmade outback tracks to join her husband Langloh Parker at Bangate Station near Walgett. The huge complex, which Langloh Parker managed, seemed more like a village than a home, and Katie distracted herself from the searing heat by recording her experiences in a journal. A pelvic injury suffered in a station accident, prevented her from producing children.

The injury ended her previous love of horse riding, but Katie threw herself into gardening and she also started to memorise and record some of the local indigenous language and customs. This research proved invaluable when she later became an author.

Both she and her husband enjoyed hosting lavish parties, but it was soon apparent that the Parkers were living beyond their means. After a second mortgage was foreclosed, Dalgety Company repossessed the property. At first Langloh Parker was retained as manager. However, after he was declared bankrupt, the couple moved to Grawin South in the state's north, where they had previously purchased a small property. By then Langloh believed his life had been a failure and he became severely depressed.

In 1896 Katie Parker had *Australian Legendary Tales* published, and this book was followed two years later by its sequel, *More Australian Legendary Tales*.

Langloh Parker died in Sydney from stomach cancer in 1903 and Katie was left a widow at the age of 47. Two years later she was sailing to England, when she met a reserved bachelor accountant named Percival Randolph Stow. After a whirlwind romance, the couple married at Westminster in London. On their return to Australia, the newly weds settled in the Adelaide suburb of Glenelg, where they became close friends with the noted artist Hans Heysen and his wife. Their daughter, Nora Heysen, later illustrated Katie's *Woggleeguy: Australian Aboriginal Legends*, which was published in 1913.

During World War I, Katie Stow became a driving force in Red Cross fund raising activities. She was a forceful but engaging personality. Katie Stow was 84 when she died at Glenelg in 1940.

FLYNN'S INSPIRATION

Myrtle Kennewell was raised in South Australia's Barossa Valley. She married a shy, young station manager named Cornelius "Con" White, at Broken Hill on 10th October 1910. Their first child, Doris, was born a year later, and soon after Con accepted a position as manager of Lake Elder Station—a remote South Australian desert area that was so forbidding that it was shunned by most indigenous people.

At first the Lake Elder homestead was unavailable, so Myrtle White coped on her own at Mirrabooka Station, where she cooked for four station hands while Con was away working. Myrtle, who had no nursing experience, had to help deliver a stranger's child, but unfortunately the baby did not survive.

Myrtle and Doris White joined Con at Lake Elder when the homestead was completed, and the hardships they faced in their new outback home were indeed formidable. The property had no telephone connection and camel train supplies to the area were unpredictable. The station was virtually a treeless desert of red sand and sandstorms were common. It was usually so hot that jellies would not set, the hot bore water supplies were almost undrinkable, it was impossible to grow vegetables and domestic help was unreliable

During her first year at Lake Elder, Myrtle became pregnant again, so a train journey for a hospital birth in the city became necessary. The trip coincided with the start of the wet season, and thick, oozy mud on the track delayed the journey to the rail head. A longer round trip became necessary, but this badly tired the horses, so the heavily pregnant Myrtle and her young daughter were forced to walk for much of the time.

To compound their problems, the buggy became bogged,

and then, when a replacement vehicle arrived, a cyclone delayed them for another three days. When they finally reached the nearest hospital, the birth of her son Alan was, thankfully, uneventful.

However, Alan proved to be a sickly child, who often suffered from tonsillitis. Furthermore, the cycle of unresolvable outback medical problems recommenced after Myrtle again became pregnant. On the trip for this birth, the White's new Ford convertible car became bogged in sand on the way to hospital. While they waited to be dug out Alan was so heat affected, that his mother feared for his life. Further on, the car became bogged again, but despair turned to joy, when a truck unexpectedly arrived. By the time they reached Broken Hill, little Alan was close to death. After he recovered, Myrtle took both him and the new baby Gary, to the sea side to recuperate from their ordeal.

The ongoing health of the new born child also became a concern. In addition, her husband, who had worked a demanding seven days a week for decades, also fell ill. The family left Noonamere after seven years and Con White took over the management of the Morden and Wonnaminta stations in the far west of NSW. By then Myrtle needed to spend two weeks in the Wilcannia hospital and during her absence young Doris competently took over the management of the new household.

The famous bushman Sidney Kidman became Con's boss at Morden and the Whites believed he failed to honour his promise to increase Con's salary. During that time Myrtle was persuaded to purchase a house in Adelaide, where her constantly ill sons received the medical attention they required.

After the family was reunited at Woonaminta, Myrtle used the regular journal entries she had scribed to write a book entitled *No Roads Go*. The publication became widely popular when it was published in 1932. In the contents, unlike the more romanticised Jeanie Gunn book titled *We of the Never-Never*, Myrtle White candidly conveyed the harsh realities of life in Australia's outback.

Around the same time, Myrtle had a chance meeting with the Reverend John Flynn. Later, in his RFDS fundraising activities, Flynn often referred to the chapter in her book that described Alan's trip across the sand hills to hospital. Myrtle also publicised the work of Flynn's Inland Mission to various audiences, but the grinding nature of Con's management work continued to take its toll on her home front.

When Sir Sidney Kidman died in 1925, Con White was managing a third station for the "cattle king", and by then the poorly paid 55-year-old man realised that he, and his 47-year-old wife, would never be able to finance their own property. The situation became even gloomier when Con contacted bronchial pneumonia and the board of directors controlling the three stations, asked him to resign as manager. Prior to falling ill, Con White had only taken six weeks leave in his 22 years of service for the company. Consequently, he believed he was poorly rewarded for his loyalty.

The disappointed couple then decided to operate a guest house at Aldgate in the Adelaide Hills, but in 1940 Con died after suffering a heart attack. Both Myrtle's sons volunteered for war service, but Gary never returned after being declared missing in action while serving in Malaya. When World War II ended Alan returned to the land, where his father had toiled for most of his working life.

In 1954 Myrtle White collaborated with illustrator Mary Durack to bring out another edition of *No Roads Go*, and the royalties from this book were donated to the RFDS. Myrtle continued to write and mange the guest house, she also published a second book entitled *For Those That Love*.

Myrtle White died aged 73 at Port Hedland Hospital on 7th July 1961, after falling ill while visiting her son Alan at his nearby property.

> *"In the slab-built zinc-roofed homestead*
> *of some lately taken run,*
> *In the tent beside the bankment of a railway just begun.*
> *In the huts on new selection, in the camps of man's unrest,*
> *On the frontiers of the Nation, live the Women of the West."*
> *("The Women of the West", George Essex Evans)*

A WRITING OUTBACK LEGEND

Jeannie Taylor grew up the leafy Melbourne suburb of Hawthorn. She enjoyed a privileged childhood and matriculated at the age of 17, after being educated at home by her mother. After completing a degree at the University of Melbourne Jeannie became a teacher. Her comfortable urban lifestyle changed dramatically soon after she met Aeneas Gunn.

At the time Gunn was employed by the Prahran Library, while he recovered from a bout of malaria, which he had contracted in WA's Kimberly Ranges. The young couple fell in love and were married shortly after Aeneas accepted the post of manager at Elsey Station.

Jeannie learned that her new home was situated 160 kilometres south of Katherine in the Northern Territory. It was one of the biggest cattle stations on the continent and measured over 5,000 hectares. Jeannie later discovered that her nearest neighbour lived 140 kilometres from Elsey Station.

The newly weds began their formidable journey by sailing from Melbourne to Port Darwin. This was followed by a long train journey. The couple then endured a five day buckboard trip over bumpy tracks to the station, where the resident stockmen were far from friendly after they met Jeannie. Some may have been shy in the company of women, but Jeannie suspected that others feared she would end their "black velvet" relationships (sexual liaisons with aboriginal woman). She was soon informed that vital supplies to the homestead only arrived once a year, and the unfamiliar landscape of the endless desert scrub, added to her overall cultural shock.

However, Jeannie immersed herself in her new environment, and she soon became fascinated with indigenous culture. She was amazed at the potent effect "pointing the bone" had on aboriginal people. Jeannie noticed that many previously healthy people lost the will to live, if "the bone" was pointed in their direction by a designated tribal elder.

The hardships in the Gunn's isolated and arduous environment were obvious, but Jeannie began to understand the strange attraction that lured people to outback Australia. Aeneas described such country as "the never-never", in other words those who live there never, never voluntarily leave it.

Jeannie deeply loved her husband, and she confided to a friend in a letter that "I would like (us) to grow old slowly together". Her romantic dreams ended abruptly when the 41-year-old Aeneas fell gravely ill on a mustering trip and died suddenly at the homestead on 16th March 1903. Malarial dysentery had snatched the love of her life from Jeannie, when Aeneas and she had only been married for 14 months.

"The best Boss ever a man struck," was the alleged comment from one aboriginal stockman, after he heard Aeneas Gunn had passed away.

A grieving Jeannie returned to Melbourne, and in 1905 *The Little Black Princess* was published. "Mrs Aeneas Gunn" was the author's name on the cover, and three years later multiple copies of *We of the Never-Never* made its appearance in retail stores. Both books are still regarded as being Australian literary classics, despite some critics claiming they conveyed paternalistic and racist attitudes.

The quote below, which is attributed to Jeannie Gunn, shows that she felt empathy towards indigenous grievances, though some of her views would not seem appropriate in today's world.

"The white man has taken the country from the black fellow…cattle killing, and at times even man killing by blacks (should) not be an offence against the white folk."

Her writing philosophy is very different in style to Myrtle White's work. White wrote about male domination in the outback, drunken orgies with indigenous women and the high suicide rates, all of which featured to some extent at Elsey Station. She also provided more graphic details about floods, droughts and other natural disasters that challenged all those who lived in the "never-never". Jeannie Gunn, however, concentrated more on positive aspects, such as the beauty of the bush landscape and the loyalty that bushmen displayed towards each other.

Jeannie Gunn at "Kilmours", East Melbourne c1935

After her father died in 1909, Jeannie Gunn travelled to Britain and Europe. Picturesque Monbulk, in the Dandenong Ranges, became a favourite haunt of hers after she returned to Melbourne, and her home there became a refuge for wounded Anzac soldiers when they returned from World War I battlefields. In 1939 Jeannie Gunn's welfare work for war veterans and their families, was recognised by the awarding of an Order of the British Empire (OBE). Her final book, published after her death, provided details about Monbulk returned soldiers.

Jeannie Gunn was aged 91 when she died in Melbourne on 9th June 1961. The tribute below was just one of many that eulogised her life.

> "A modest, gentle, courageous lady. Some will remember her for her books and others for her unremitting service to those who fought for Australia."

In 1982 *We of the Never-Never* was made into a film. A replica of Elsey Station, situated at Manaranka Springs Resort, is now visited by the general public. The original station was returned to local aboriginal people.

The estate of Jeannie Gunn (OBE) was divided up between the many causes and charities she supported throughout her long life.

HARDLY A TROPICAL PARADISE

Evelyn Evans was aged 21, when she and a female travelling companion arrived in Sydney. There Evelyn met Charlie Maunsell, who was so smitten by her that he proposed marriage within a week. Before accepting, Evelyn waited for parental permission to be conveyed from England after which she began a hazardous journey that transported her to a dangerous and disease infected area of north Queensland.

After travelling by paddle steamer from Brisbane to the then ramshackle port of Cairns, Evelyn was reunited with Charles, who had recently been appointed manager of Mt Mulgrave, one of the state's largest cattle stations. Charles and Evelyn Maunsell were married on 21st July 1912. Some wedding guests were sceptical about how the young immigrant bride would cope with life in the wilds of the tropics.

"This English girl will never stick it out," was one alleged opinion.

Evelyn's early experiences would have indeed tested her marriage commitment. Her encounters with some River aborigines have already been mentioned in Chapter Two of this book and she experienced many other harrowing problems also.

Soon after she arrived Evelyn became pregnant, but a serious bout of malaria nearly ended her life and she suffered a miscarriage after travelling over 100 kilometres on horseback to Cairns Hospital, where she occupied a hospital bed for 14 days. She continued to suffered periodic malaria attacks for the rest of her life.

Once she recovered sufficiently the resilient Evelyn Maunsell returned to Mt Mulgrave determined to showed that she would indeed "stick it out". She commenced growing a tropical garden and she and local indigenous women became involved in knitting scarves and sending food parcels to the World War I battlefront. She also nursed Tim Evans, her war traumatised brother, when he recuperated from the horrors of war at Mt Mulgrave. At the same time, Evelyn had to cope with her own grief, as her second pregnancy also ended in miscarriage, during the wet season of 1917.

Financially the Maunsells prospered on the cattle station, and they were able to purchase a 50 acre dairy farm on the Atherton Tablelands near Cairns. Charlie received further rewards after Mt Mulgrave was auctioned, with the grateful owners presenting him with racehorses and heifers as a bonus for his skilful management. Evelyn continued to display her versatility, erecting fences around the Atherton property, when Charlie's work took him away from the dairy farm.

The lure of the "never-never" attracted the Maunsells again, and they departed from the Atherton Tablelands and took over the management of Wroxham Park, one of the biggest and most productive cattle stations in the country. The homestead there had been well maintained and Evelyn became responsible for operating the station store, while Charlie enjoyed maintaining and improving the enormous 596,000 hectare property.

Once more he proved to be a successful manager and the appreciative owners granted his application for 12 months leave on full pay, so he and Evelyn could travel to England to reunite with her family. It proved to be an unexpectedly productive trip, as Evelyn fell pregnant again. The couple enjoyed visiting England, Ireland, Canada and the United States and on 8th May 1922 Ronald Maunsell was born soon after they returned to Wroxham Park.

After their time on the station ended, Charlie and Evelyn

returned to the Atherton Tablelands dairy farm for 20 years and they later operated a sheep station near Longreach. Their son Ron married soon after returning from World War II action and in later years this father of three daughters served as a Senator in Federal Parliament until 1961.

Charlie lived to be 87 before he died in 1970, while Evelyn Maunsell was 89 when she passed away in 1977.

A CHAMPION OF INDIGENOUS AUSTRALIANS

Daisy May Bates

During her long, productive and controversial life, Daisy May Bates became a noted journalist, author, amateur anthropologist and a strong supporter of indigenous languages and culture.

At the age of 18, she left the Irish capital of Dublin after being involved in an alleged sex scandal when she was employed as a governess. By 1881 Daisy Bates (whose actual name may have been Margaret Dwyer) arrived in Townsville as a free immigrant and soon took up a post as a governess at Fanning Downs Station.

On 13th March 1884, Daisy married "Breaker" Morant, a charismatic if infamous character who was later controversially executed while serving with British forces in South Africa's Boer War. The marriage with Morant did not survive long, partly because he neglected to pay for the wedding! Morant was also accused of stealing livestock from the station, which further strained their relationship. Bates and Morant never divorced, but she became involved in a long term de facto relationship with Jack Bates, a former sailor and the son of a wealthy London family.

Daisy Bates spent time in England after 1894, before returning to Australia five years later as an investigative journalist for the *London Times*. The focus of her assignment was the investigation of cruelty allegations from Western Australian settlers, towards aboriginal people living on the Nullabour Plain. The welfare of indigenous Australians soon became a life long commitment for Daisy Bates.

For the next 35 years she devoted her energies to publicising their languages, cultures and problems to the wider world. Bates lived in tents in various small aboriginal settlements on the edge of the Nullabour. Travellers on the Transcontinental Railway (a service that links Adelaide to Perth) grew accustomed to seeing an eccentric white woman, dressed primly in Edwardian style, standing beside fearsome looking aboriginal warriors at small railway sidings. Daisy Bates usually wore fashionable boots, her face was covered with a veil, and she always wore gloves. It was also believed she carried pistols in her belt, to safeguard her welfare.

Bates was instrumental in setting up camps to feed, clothe and nurse needy aborigines, and she often used her own income to finance welfare initiatives. She also fought against the concept of assimilating indigenous people into white society, and campaigned against the sexual exploitation of aboriginal women. Bates was contemptuous towards half-caste aborigines, allegedly claiming that "the only good half-caste is a dead one." She also strongly declared that cannibalism was rife in some indigenous groups, a frequently expressed opinion that created a storm of controversy.

At the age of 36, Daisy moved to the northern part of the state, where she resided at the Beagle Bay Mission in Broome. There she started to record the results of her research and compile a dictionary of local indigenous dialects. Daisy, Jack and their son Arnold Bates then embarked on a six month droving trip from Broome to Perth. The relationship between Daisy and Jack deteriorated on the long journey and they seperated soon after arriving in Perth. After 1902, Daisy Bates spent much of her time researching in remote areas of Western Australia and South Australia. From that time onwards she became increasingly involved in acrimonious debates with other scholars and authorities.

She accused Professor Alfred Ratcliffe Brown of plagiarising her findings. Bates also claimed that gender discrimination applied, when her application to become Protector of Aborigines in the Northern Territory was unsuccessful. In 1914 she subsequently became Honorary Protector at Eucla in South Australia, from where she continued to contribute regularly to newspapers, magazines and academic societies.

Public recognition of her work was provided in 1933 by the Federal Government, who appointed her to be an aboriginal adviser. A year later Daisy Bates was honoured with a Companion of the British Empire (CBE) award. She then resided for some time in a tent on the Murray River, where she continued to cause furore by writing about the prevalence of cannibalism among various indigenous groups.

She spent the final years of her life in Adelaide and unsuccessfully attempted to revive a broken relationship with her son, who had emigrated to New Zealand. Daisy Bates lived to the age of 91, before she passed away in 1951.

Daisy Bates with a group of Aboriginal women, c1911

SOME MODERN OUTBACK HEROINES

Faith Bander

Faith Bandar was born in 1919 and was one of eight children. Her father had previously only been 13-years-of age when he became a "blackbird" (kidnapped Pacific Islander). He was abducted from his New Hebrides home and forced to work on sugar cane plantations in northern Australia.

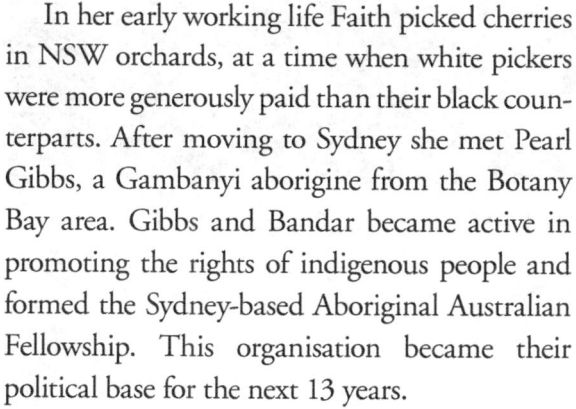

In her early working life Faith picked cherries in NSW orchards, at a time when white pickers were more generously paid than their black counterparts. After moving to Sydney she met Pearl Gibbs, a Gambanyi aborigine from the Botany Bay area. Gibbs and Bandar became active in promoting the rights of indigenous people and formed the Sydney-based Aboriginal Australian Fellowship. This organisation became their political base for the next 13 years.

Faith Bandar became the NSW campaign director for the "Yes" vote to provide equal franchise for aboriginal people, a landmark outcome that was achieved in the 1967 Federal elections. In that same year the Aboriginal Australian Fellowship was renamed the Federal Council for the Advancement of Aborigines and Torres Strait Islanders (FCAATSI). Following the referendum success, the group declined somewhat in public popularity, after it assertively pursued the goal for aborigines to promote their own distinct culture.

Bandar continued campaigns for aboriginal causes and within the FCAATSI, she strived to gain a racial mix in the executive leadership group.

Beagle Bay Mission north of Broome, c1964

Kathleen Ruska was born on Minjerriba (Stradbroke Island) in 1920 and became a noted poet, author, actress, artist and campaigner for aboriginal rights.

Kath left school at the age of 13 and worked as a domestic servant. She was self educated and wished to train as a nurse, but believes her application was unsuccessful because of her aboriginality. Following this setback, Kath volunteered for army service and in 1942 she married a fellow aborigine named Bruce Walker. The marriage produced two sons and Kath Walker raised them as a single parent soon after World War II ended.

Between 1961 and 1970, Kath Walker achieved national prominence when she became Queensland secretary of the Council for the Advancement of Aborigines and Torres Strait Islanders (CAATSI). During that time she also wrote poetry, and, by the time Kath Walker was in her 40s, she became the first published aboriginal poet, with the anthology *We Are Going* appearing in book shops. All available copies sold out within three days, which rivalled the works of the famous CJ Dennis in popularity.

More examples of Kath Walker's poetry were included in three other published anthologies. She also wrote many children's books, including *The Rainbow Serpent*, which was co-authored by her son Vivian (later changed to Kabul). The lines quoted below promote the hope for understanding and peace between black and white people of Australia, a dominant theme in her writing.

> *"But I'll tell instead of brave and fine,*
> *When lives of black and white entwine*
> *And men in brotherhood combine;*
> *This would I tell you, son of mine."*

Kath Walker

Kath Walker was a passionate political activist and she was strongly involved with aboriginal welfare groups such as the Tribal Council, Arts Board, Housing Committee and Advancement League. Prior to the successful 1967 referendum, Walker was a prominent spokesperson for the "Yes" vote, but she later became disillusioned with the pace of needed reform. Her disenchantment extended to Australia's 1988 Bicentennial celebrations (an event she boycotted) and she also returned the MBE medal she was awarded in 1970.

The acclaimed poet later returned to her childhood base of Stradbroke Island, where she hoped to build an aboriginal museum. However, she was forced to live in caravans or tents, when the government refused permission to construct a permanent building. In recent years Kath Walker changed her name to Oodgeroo Noonuccal. She remained firmly committed to promoting aboriginal culture and education, until she passed away in 1993 at the age of 72.

Lois "Lowitja" O'Donoghue (AC, CBE, DSG) is not a typical retired public servant. She was the inaugural President of the now dissolved Aboriginal and Torres Strait Islander Commission (ASTIC) and she was named Australian of the Year in both 1984 and 1990. In 1976 O'Donoghue became the recipient of an Order of Australia medal, an award that recognised her dedicated work in the field of aboriginal welfare.

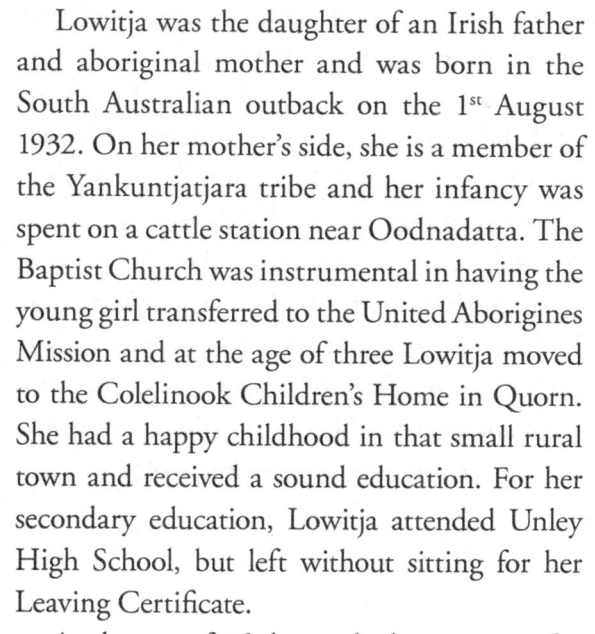

Lois "Lowitja" O'Donoghue

Lowitja was the daughter of an Irish father and aboriginal mother and was born in the South Australian outback on the 1st August 1932. On her mother's side, she is a member of the Yankuntjatjara tribe and her infancy was spent on a cattle station near Oodnadatta. The Baptist Church was instrumental in having the young girl transferred to the United Aborigines Mission and at the age of three Lowitja moved to the Colelinook Children's Home in Quorn. She had a happy childhood in that small rural town and received a sound education. For her secondary education, Lowitja attended Unley High School, but left without sitting for her Leaving Certificate.

At the age of 16 she worked as a nanny for three years at Victor Harbour. After qualifying as a nurse she was stationed at Royal Adelaide Hospital until 1961 and then spent a year working with the Baptist Church in India. In 1962 she was employed as an aboriginal liaison and welfare officer with the government and was stationed for some time at Coober Pedy. Lowitja O'Donoghue then severed her connections with the state public service and served in various administrative roles with non-government organisations. In 1979 she married Gordon Smart, who was a medical orderly, but he died after only 12 years of marriage.

In December 1992 Lowitja O'Donoghue became the first Australian aborigine to address the United Nations General Assembly, during the launch of the International Year of Indigenous People. She became passionately involved in highlighting the plight of many outback aborigines who formed part of the stolen generation, a group taken from their biological parents at an early age and placed under European foster care. In 2007 the then Prime Minister, John Howard, received trenchant criticism from O'Donoghue, because of his perceived lack of remorse about this much debated issue.

February 3rd 2008, was therefore a proud day for Lowitja, and those surviving aborigines who had been plucked from their homes. On that day, the new Prime Minister, Kevin Rudd, implemented a "national day of sorrow", when he, and other Federal parliamentarians, publicly apologised to aboriginal families for past government wrongs to the stolen generation of Australians.

A STAR OF THE SCREEN

Ngarla Kunoth Monk and her co-actor Robert Tudawali, became the first aboriginal film stars to appear in lead roles in a major Australian film. The film was called *Jedda*, the name given to a fictitious young aboriginal girl who was raised by Europeans on an outback cattle station.

In the script, the girl is lured away from a comfortable and safe homestead by Marbuck, a wild young man, whose traditional indigenous culture is far removed from the cloistered European world that Jedda has known.

Marbuck becomes an outcast in both black and white societies, after escaping from legal custody while facing a charge of murder. The elders of his tribe sing him to death and at the end of the film the crazed fugitive and his lover Jedda, jump to their deaths from a high cliff top.

The movie, with the mysterious grandeur of Northern Territory scenery in the background, made a major impact on Australian and international audiences. Charles and Edna Chauvel were the film's producers; they recruited the two young aborigines to the cast, after interviewing many potential candidates.

Tudawali and Kunoth became Australian equivalents of Hollywood stars. Only three European actors had minor roles in the film and at least eight different indigenous cultures were meaningfully presented on screen for the first time to predominantly European audiences. *Jedda* also revealed the importance of station hands in the successful management of large outback properties.

Some critics were less than complimentary about the film's themes though few criticised the performances of the two aboriginal lead actors. Tudawali acted in one more major film, but *Jedda* was the only film Kunoth ever appeared in. The film was fortuitously presented to the public in 1955, as a year later the advent of television into Australian homes, restricted the development of the Australian film industry for many years.

Rosalie Ngarla Kunoth was first discovered by the Chauvels when she was a 14-year-old student at St Mary's Anglican Hostel in Alice Springs. After *Jedda* was filmed she briefly returned to St Mary's, before helping in the care of underprivileged children with the Melbourne-based Sisters of the Holy Name. Kunoth decided that welfare work was her life's calling and at the age of 20, she pledged her vows of dedication to the Order and received the title of Sister Rosalie. Twelve years later she left the Order to take up a position with the Department of Aboriginal Affairs. During her years in the public service, Kunoth married Bill Monk, a white retailer of confectionery goods.

Her 20-year stay in Melbourne produced seven children and the large family group then moved to the Red Centre. In the NT, Ngarla Kunoth Monk devoted herself to fostering many aboriginal children. She also became involved in projects that aimed to improve the education, housing and health of indigenous Australians. Ngarla Kunoth Monk became a candidate for the NT Parliament in 1979, when traditional lands were threatened by a dam project, but her attempt to become a Parliamentarian was unsuccessful.

In 1993 Ngarla returned to Utopia, the place where she was born. Since returning to her roots, Kunoth Monk has continued her welfare work in this isolated community, which is situated 250 kilometres north-east of Alice Springs. She has been Chancellor of the Bachelor Institute of Indigenous Tertiary Education and was interviewed by Andrew Denton on the ABC *Elders* program. In March 2007 Ngarla Kunoth Monk was presented with the NT Tribute to Women Award.

CHAPTER SIX:
HIGH ACHIEVER ON TRACKS FURTHER OUT

FATHER OF THE INLAND

Until the late 1920s, Australian outback people faced huge problems if serious illness or life threatening injuries disturbed the normal course of their lives. Health care was totally inadequate—at times there were only two doctors available to service an area of nearly 700,000 square miles.

The medical crises faced by Atalanta Bradshaw, Katie Parker, Myrtle White, Aeneas Gunn, Evelyn Maunsell and others have already been documented in previous chapters of this book. Few cases were more horrific, however, than the drama filled 1917 incident that ultimately had fatal consequences for Jimmy Darcy.

Darcy was a Western Australian stockman, who ruptured his bladder and was taken by friends on a 12-hour journey to the tiny township of Halls Creek. There Mr F.W. Tuckett, the local postmaster, unsuccessfully attempted to contact doctors in both Wyndham and Derby. He was finally forced to rely on Morse code assistance from Dr Holland, a medico in far

Reverend John Flynn

off Perth. Tuckett, who had some knowledge of basic first aid procedures, rendered the seriously ill Darcy insensible with the aid of copious amounts of whiskey. He then strapped his intoxicated patient to the post office counter and performed two pen knife operations on him.

Meanwhile, Dr Holland departed from Perth for a two day rescue journey by boat, car, horse drawn carriage and foot, to the isolated hamlet of Halls Creek. Unfortunately, by the time the conscientious medico reached his destination, Jimmy Darcy had died. Ironically, it was not the ruptured bladder or the traumatic surgery that caused the stockman's demise but a previously undiagnosed malarial condition and a ruptured abscess in his appendix.

The person who revolutionised health care in inland Australia was the Reverend John Flynn, who was born in the Victorian gold mining town of Moliagul on 25th November 1880. After beginning his working life as student-teacher John Flynn changed his vocation and trained for the ministry. During his years as a divinity student he gained worthwhile experience at a shearer's mission, and in 1910 John Flynn published a book titled *Bushman's Companion*.

In 1911 Flynn began life as an ordained clergyman in the North Flinders Ranges. Oodnadatta was included in his vast parish and it was there he was appointed as the Superintendent of the

Presbyterian General Assembly. Flynn also helped to establish the Oodnadatta Nursing Hostel. From the early stages of his ministry, John Flynn showed that he was both an impressive speaker and an attentive listener.

Flynn soon realised that outback welfare structures needed to be initiated and that community groups needed to take responsibility for coordinating their own safety procedures. He became personally responsible for the design of many hostel buildings, and his managerial experience later proved beneficial in the implementation of a flying doctor service.

Between 1913 and 1927 the Reverend Flynn published an influential outback magazine called the *Inlander*, which highlighted many problems of outback Australia. Aboriginal issues was one area of concern frequently addressed.

A chance meeting with World War I veteran Clifford Peel, introduced Flynn to the concept of an aeroplane solution for outback health services. Before Peel died in a 1918 field of battle, he communicated his ideas to Flynn, after hearing him speak at a public meeting. The enterprising Reverend then collaborated with a young electronic expert named Alfred Traeger, and following their discussions Traeger invented the pedal radio. In the mid 1920s, this invention was gradually distributed to stations and missions around Cloncurry. The concept of aeroplanes facilitating health care began to resonate nationally.

The Air Medical Service (AMS) began on 10th May 1928. It received significant financial support from the industrialists Sir W. Hudson Fysh, who founded the Qantas company, and H.V. Mackay. Qantas provided the AMS with its first plane—a De Haviland DH 50 dubbed "Victory", and during the first year of operation, users of the service were charged two shillings for every mile covered for medical visits—a sum that grateful outback clients gladly paid.

The AMS was heavily reliant on public financial support, especially during the war years and in the time of the Great Depression. However, by 1934, new bases had been established at Wyndham, Port Hedland, Kalgoorlie, Broken Hill, Alice Springs, Meekatharra, Charters Towers and Charleville. Myra Blanch, a nurse who became one of the first "Flying Sisters", introduced a body chart, which became much used in station homesteads. Areas on the printed body were clearly numbered, which resulted in doctor's instructions (similar to the example below) being conveyed in radio messages.

"Rub ointment 46 onto number 11 before I arrive".

Today the Royal Flying Doctor Service (RFDS) has been greatly extended. Four wheel drive services are now available and emergency first aid sites have been put in place. Other features of this much acclaimed service include transport to hospitals, satellite phones and portable radio advice, regular liaisons with rural doctors in remote areas and inter-hospital transfers. By the beginning of the 21st century, the RFDS served a population of approximately 750,000 people, scattered over an area equivalent in size to all of Western Europe.

The Reverend John Flynn's face is now depicted on the Australian $50 note, and the roving outback missionary was honoured in various other ways for his outstanding contributions to health services in isolated areas. In the church hierarchy, he became Moderator of the Presbyterian Church of Australia and he was Superintendent of the Inland Mission for 39 years. Flynn also became a recipient of an Order of the British Empire (OBE) award.

Nearly a decade after his death, Flynn's reputation unexpectedly became the focus of controversy, following the 1972 publication of Dr Charles Duguid's book *Doctor and the Aborigines*.

High Achiever on Tracks Further Out

Duguid and others claimed that Flynn became indifferent to aboriginal problems and that the Oodnadatta hostel refused to provide necessary health care for local indigenous people. Such accusations have been vehemently repudiated by Flynn's many supporters.

Flynn married his long serving secretary, Jean Baird, in 1932 and she survived her 71-year-old husband, who died of cancer in 1951.

Padre Kingsley Partridge provided the following tribute to "Flynn of the inland" at his funeral service.

> "Across the lonely places of the land he planted kindness, and from the hearts of those who call those places home, he gathered love."

John Flynn was buried at the foot of Mt Gillen. Five years later, the John Flynn Memorial Church was opened in nearby Alice Springs.

Royal Flying Doctor Service at Ivanhoe airstrip, NSW 1982

127

THE WIRE MAN

Alfred Traeger speaking into a pedal powered wireless transmitter, c1935

Gilbert and Sullivan, Paul and Marie Curie, Lerner and Lowe...there have been many impressive partnerships throughout history. Flynn and Traeger were another productive duo.

Alfred Hemann Traeger was the son of a Victorian farmer. By the age of 12 he invented a telephone set for the family farm, which could communicate spoken messages between the woolshed and the homestead. It was almost inevitable that Alf Traeger became a qualified electrical engineer. He also developed a deep love for the outback terrain and for the people who lived in isolated areas.

A chance meeting with the Reverend John Flynn in 1926 proved to be productive. Flynn challenged the 31-year old Traeger to develop a radio communication system that would link outback homesteads with a central control point. The talented electrical engineer "delivered the goods".

In 1929 Traeger developed a battery operated machine that sent and received Morse code messages. Traeger continued to experiment and was soon able to provide permanent energy with his invention of the pedal radio. Pedal power provided the energy requirements when messages were transmitted. Communication became easier for participants, after Traeger devised a key board that transmitted Morse code messages.

John Flynn had the overall vision for improving communication in the vast Australian wilderness, but it was the electronic genius of Alf Traeger that turned a dream into a reality.

THE MONEY MAN

"...Old Peter'll say 'Let's pass him through';
There's many a good thing he used to do,
Good-hearted things that no one knew,
That's T.Y.S.O.N."

This is the last stanza of a tribute poem about James Tyson, which was penned by the famous writer A.B. "Banjo" Paterson. Tyson was the son of a convict mother. However, the man later dubbed "Hungry" by the *Bulletin*, overcame his humble beginnings and became one of the wealthiest pastoralists Australia has ever known. It is estimated, that when Tyson died, he left an estate valued at approximately two million pounds (at least $8,000,000).

James Tyson was born at Narellan in central NSW and was engaged in various occupations during the nomadic years of his youth. At Appin he was a farmhand and he also worked as an apprentice boot maker and a pastoral labourer around Yass.

In 1846 James Tyson took over a run near the junction of the Murrumbidgee and Lachlan Rivers and soon after he became a partner in a butchery shop near the goldfields of Bendigo. It proved to be a lucrative purchase, as three years later he sold the business for an estimated value of eighty thousand pounds ($300,000). Tyson used part of the proceeds to purchase three properties near Deniliquin, which he soon improved by adding fences, water tanks and irrigation channels.

Tyson continued to be a wealth magnet. His late brother John left him a generous amount of money in his estate, and after James Tyson sold his Deniliquin assets, he moved back to the Lachlan River area. By 1898 James Tyson held more than five million acres of land; over 350,000 acres of this acreage were freehold assets. Tyson also owned five livestock stations in NSW, one in Victoria and 11 in Queensland along with properties in Toowoomba, Brisbane and Hay. On his properties he bred and fattened stock for metropolitan markets.

Between 1893 and 1898 James Tyson served as a member in the Queensland Legislative Assembly, His short-lived political career was unspectacular—during his five year tenure James Tyson only delivered one short speech in the state's Lower House. He did, however, become involved in land tenure reforms and gave generously to various charities.

James Tyson

James Tyson remained a bachelor all his life, and allegedly never smoked, swore or consumed alcohol in any form. He passed away in 1898 at the age of 79.

THE CATTLE KING

He ran away from his boyhood home on a one-eyed horse with only five shillings in his pocket, but Sidney Kidman later became a millionaire and one of the most influential figures the Australian outback has ever known

Sid Kidman was probably born near Adelaide and his father died when he was aged six. His mother's second husband was a drunken bully called Starr, and Sid, together with his brothers George, Fred, Tom and Sackville, all left home at an early age.

After fleeing from his depressing domestic situation, the teenage Sidney found work around the Barrier Ranges in "the corner country" of NSW, where he later purchased many properties. His first employer was a landless bushman named George Raines. During that stage of his life, Sidney shared a dugout with an aboriginal lad called Billy, and under his guidance Kidman became so skilled in bushcraft, that Raines sometimes used him as an outback guide. Sidney respected Billy's expertise and in later years he frequently used aboriginal help to guide him to outback destinations.

Sidney Kidman then worked for over a year as a rouseabout with his brothers George, Fred and Sackville at Mt Gipps Station, which was later named Broken Hill, when rich deposits of silver, lead and zinc were discovered. Sid was sacked from his employment there, after asking for a rise in pay. He then worked as a stockman for "German Charlie". His place of work was later described as being "a wild frontier outpost". The frugal Sidney saved enough money in this primitive environment to purchase a bullock team and was soon employing others.

Kidman then became involved with carting supplies to isolated areas of NSW, Victoria and South Australia, before he and Sackville established a butcher's shop in Cobar, after copper was discovered there in the early 1870s. Sackville also became the driving force in a highly successful Broken Hill butchery business. There he became a popular local identity, and Broken Hill came to a standstill on the day of his funeral. One local station owner emotionally declared that, "If there was one man in the world, to whom I would give my last drop of heart's blood, it was Sack Kidman."

The loss of Sack shocked Sidney, but by then his burgeoning business interests were making him a wealthy man. A coaching transport business in Cobar (which became similar in scope to the famous Cobb and Co enterprise) combined with his investments in livestock markets, helped to further build Sidney Kidman's business interests.

In 1856 he purchased Owen Springs Cattle Station on the Hugh River, south-west of Alice Springs. It was the first step in an ambitious long-term scheme for Kidman.

The man admirers later dubbed "the cattle king" aimed to buy a chain of stations that would stretch south, in a nearly continuous line, from well-watered tropical land around the Gulf of Carpentaria, through Queensland to Broken Hill, before finishing close to Adelaide. Kidman would rely on water supplies from Coopers Creek, as well as the Georgina and Diamitina Rivers, to service his properties, even in times of drought.

He revealed details of his vision to Harry Peck, the author of *Memoirs of a Stockman*.

> "Give me the country in western Queensland, where a bullock will fatten on herbage in three months, and (when) rain follows a dry spell, the soil will grow feed sweet and lasting produce."

Kidman also spoke to Peck about his faith in the outback flood cycle, asserting that good feed from the water was available all along the river system.

"Much of it retained its nutrition, even after it (the river) dried... Wherever the flood waters have reached the country, it greens up".

Kidman was influenced in his vision by a South Australian school teacher named Isobel Wright, whom he married on 30th June 1885. The couple produced three daughters and a son and had a very happy marriage.

The couple soon realised that none of the inland rivers flowed into the sea. They all sank into the sandy flood plains of the west and formed an inland sea under the mostly parched land. Flood waters from the north could fill the dry creek beds of the interior without a drop of inland rain falling. Overall, Sidney Kidman envisioned a grassy highway where most others saw sandy wastelands, and the back corridor of his connecting stations, would potentially deliver handsome profits at the meat markets in South Australia.

By the 1890s "the cattle king" had bought a string of stations that followed the Overland Telegraph line, which encompassed Fitzroy River and Victoria River Downs, to Wilpena Station in the Flinders Ranges. This strategy enabled the cagy bushman to sell stock when the prices were at their highest. Consequently Kidman remained viable when other landholders failed during the 1890s Great Depression and the searing drought of 1902. By the start of World War I, Sidney Kidman owned land that rivalled the size of Victoria.

During the Great War, Kidman was a generous benefactor to the allied cause. Fighter planes and other military equipment were financed, he donated one thousand pounds, a cattle station and a Kapunda home to the Salvation Army. After the Kapunda residence became a district secondary school, Sidney Kidman's generosity was rewarded with a knighthood.

Opinions about Sir Sidney Kidman varied greatly. He was renowned for being a martinet about efficiency, even in regard to matters of minor importance. It was rumoured that he sacked men who lit cigarettes with matches, if the option of a camp fire was available to them. His supporters maintained that Sidney Kidman was "a rough diamond", whose straight talking ways could be trusted. They remember him as an affable man, who never drank, smoked or swore and described him as an excellent judge of people. They also praised Kidman's generosity, both as an employer and as a benefactor.

Kidman also had detractors. To people like Langloh Parker, he seemed a ruthless employer, and overall (his sternest critics claim) Sir Sidney Kidman exploited rather than developed outback pastoral areas.

Kidman was probably the only man on Earth who could ride for around one thousand kilometres without trespassing on another person's property, and at the time of his death he either controlled, or partly owned, 68 different cattle stations. In his later years Kidman seemed to enjoy his celebrity status, with his 1932 70th birthday celebrations being described as "Australia's largest individual party".

Sir Sidney Kidman was aged 73 when he died in 1935.

DRESSED FOR THE PART

RM Williams

Reginald Murray Williams, commonly referred to as "RM", is another "rags to riches" legend of the outback. RM was virtually a swagman, until he created a popular style of bush-wear clothing that rapidly transformed him to millionaire status.

Williams was brought up near South Australia's Flinders Ranges, where his father raised horses. He later described those childhood years as being "the horse and buggy days, when Mum had to cook, wash and iron, without electricity (or convenient) water supplies".

RM left school in Adelaide at the age of 15, to pursue a life of adventure in the outback. His first job was assisting in the construction of a stone water tank in the desert and at nights he taught himself to read by the light of a camp fire. Between the ages of 18 and 21, RM Williams worked as a camel driver for a missionary in isolated areas where there were no roads, trails or maps to guide them. They often lived with aboriginal groups and learned how to survive in the outback. During those years, RM was taught how to plait using strands of kangaroo leather. He married Thelma Mitchell and returned to the Flinders Ranges. The couple lived a pioneer existence during their early married life and RM later recalled how "we used to grind our own wheat and cook rabbits and kangaroos", which became regular meals

High Achiever on Tracks Further Out

for Williams, his wife and their family of six children.

A chance meeting with a man dubbed "Dollar Mick", dramatically changed the life of the struggling family. Dollar Mick showed RM Williams how to make leather bridles, pack saddles and boots. Later, when Williams' son, Ian, urgently required eye treatment in hospital, a desperate RM persuaded the famous Sidney Kidman to purchase some of his saddles. With part of the sale proceeds he began a leather manufacturing business, which operated out of his father's garage in Adelaide.

The new enterprise experienced its share of teething problems. Williams was soon plunged into debt after borrowing money to further expand the business, but he remained undeterred. Despite his financial problems, he persuaded a group of other adventurous businessmen to join with him in the purchase of a Tennant Creek gold mine, for the formidable sum of seventy-two thousand pounds, (at least $500,000 in today's currency). In this case fortune favoured the brave, as "Nobles Nob" became one of the richest small gold mines in the country.

"We made many, many millions," Williams later confided.

Before long, however, the trappings of a millionaire's life became unattractive for the rugged bushman.

"I couldn't handle prosperity," admitted RM "(so) I went back to where I belonged." Williams rejected city life and returned to "tracks further out", where he became involved in rejuvenating a run down cattle station. By then his first marriage had collapsed and after RM remarried, he became the father of three more children. He also published five anthologies of his own poems, and helped establish the Stockman's Hall of Fame at Longreach in Queensland.

Today the Williams family own many outback properties, and the bush-wear business empire that RM founded continues to flourish. The bush legend was 95 when he died in his weatherboard home on Queensland's Darling Downs in 2003.

137

STRAIGHT AS A GUN BARREL

Len Beadell surveyor explorer and author, c1988

From 1947 until the 1960s, Len Beadell became responsible for both the surveying and the subsequent later construction of a gigantic road. It commenced at the Woomera Rocket Range north of Port Augusta and ended at the eighty mile beach near the north-western coastal town of Broome.

The enormous undertaking encompassed over one and a half million square kilometres of land, dominated by sand dunes, Spinifex and mulga, over some of the most confronting deserts on the planet. Water, and any semblance of roads or settlements, was virtually non-existent and even the most adventurous local aborigines would not venture beyond the fringes of this forbidding territory.

The Woomera (Aboriginal term for a spear thrower) Rocket Range was one of the largest science laboratories on Earth. Beadell's challenge was to provide road access to and from this vital institution. Overall his job prescription was to map and construct 7,000 kilometres of road and he was forced to rely on bush skills that few others could match.

Fortunately Beadell had a strong background in bushcraft, which he first developed during his childhood scouting expeditions near Sydney. In his adult years he trained as a surveyor with the Government Water Board and during World

War II he served with the Army Survey Corps in New Guinea. Shortly after the war ended, Beadell was invited to help establish a site for the future Woomera Rocket Range.

Once his reconnaissance work began, the Beadell survey group would usually adopt the following procedure. Len would drive his vehicle into unknown territory, and use flares or hand mirror messages when he wished the bulldozer drivers and cherry pickers to continue on. The direction he usually followed was gun barrel straight, though Beadell would include bends in his surveys, if aboriginal sites or birds habitats were threatened.

At times, death seemed perilously close for the intrepid leader. In one incident (500 kilometres from the nearest settlement) Beadell was stranded with a broken axle on his vehicle for three weeks. When a rescue team finally found him, the first comment to the relieved leader from one wag in his team was, "Excuse me, but do you know anyone here who needs help?"

Beadell himself was renowned for his keen sense of humour, a quality sorely needed when flat tyres, lack of suitable drinking water and petrol vaporisation from vehicles became constant problems. The heat was so intense that on one occasion the nails in Beadell's boots became loosened and the team was often forced to start the day at dawn with a "Pelican's breakfast"—a drink of water and a look around. Beadell became unusually versatile in his skills, acting as the group's barber, mechanic, first aid officer and dentist.

The first leg of the Woomera project was completed in 1956 and covered 600 kilometres from Victory Downs to near Alice Springs. The second stage traversed the dreaded terrain known as the Gibson Desert (named in honour of the explorer Alfred Gibson, a member the 1862 Giles expedition who vanished without trace during an arduous journey into the unknown).

Finally, in the decade between 1953 and 1963 an imposing

7,000 kilometres of road was laid, it was appropriately named the Gun Barrel Highway. The road was usually perfectly straight for every 48 kilometres and after it was completed Beadell, despite fading health, continued working on the Woomera Road construction until 1963. He married Anne and the two of them enjoyed treks into the outback after the care of their three children became less onerous.

In 1959 Len Beadell was awarded the British Empire Medal, and the Order of Australia (OA) medal was bequeathed to him in 1989. Len revealed his versatility by becoming the author of seven books, which included his own excellent cartoons. The pioneer surveyor also regularly lectured to students, before he died from a heart condition in 1995.

The Gun Barrel Highway

THE MAN OF IRON

Langley Frederick "Lang" Hancock achieved both fame, and to a certain degree infamy, during his eventful life. Considerable wealth and recognition came his way in 1952, after he discovered the world's largest iron ore deposits. However, controversy followed in 1985 after his third marriage to a woman who was 39 years younger. This union led to bitter legal conflicts between Hancock's new wife, Rose, and the iron ore magnate's daughter, Gina Rinehart, after Lang Hancock died in 1992.

He was born into a Western Australian landowning family and attended the prestigious Hale School in Perth. Prior to starting secondary school, Hancock was raised at Ashburton and Mulga Downs Stations, which were isolated cattle holdings belonging to the Hancock family. Later Hancock returned to the outback to help his father manage the properties.

As a young boy, Hancock discovered asbestos deposits at Wittenboom Gorge and the family began mining operations there in 1938. In his early adult years, Hancock owned 49% of the Wittenboom holdings, but a 1948 dispute with the CSR Company caused him to offload his shares. In future years, this mine became the centre of much controversy, after many asbestos related diseases came to light.

At the age of 26, Hancock married 21-year-

Above: Mining magnate Lang Hancock, c1969
Bellow: Gina Rinehart

old Susan Maley, and the couple resided at the Mulga Downs homestead for many years, before Susan returned permanently to Perth. His old school mate, E.A. "Peter" Wright then took over the management of the property.

During World War II, Hancock rose to the rank of sergeant while serving in a militia unit. Soon after the war concluded he married Hope Nicholas, who became the mother of his only child, Georgina Hope "Gina" Hancock. Lang and Hope were married for 35 years, before she passed away in 1983.

November 16th 1952, was the day that dramatically changed Hancock's life. While he was flying with Hope in their light aeroplane from Nunyerry to Perth, bad weather forced them to detour low over the barren Pilbara area. As they flew over the rugged ranges, he noticed something unusually exciting about the rock formations in the gorges above the Turner River.

"It looked to me like solid iron…I was particularly alerted by the rusty colour," Lang later recalled.

The enterprising Hancock wasted no time investigating his chance discovery. With prospector Ken McCamey, he followed the seam for approximately 112 kilometres and the pair soon realised that the Pilbara contained enough iron ore to supply the entire world.

He lobbied furiously for almost a decade to have government embargos on the export of iron ore lifted and in 1961 he was at last successful. Hancock then publicly revealed his discovery and staked his claim. The Rio Tinto Company agreed to develop the find and both Hancock and his business partner Peter Wright, shared annual royalties of $25,000,000 from the discovery.

By 1990 Hancock was estimated to possess assets valued at approximately $125,000,000; his daughter Gina was also listed among Australia's ten wealthiest people. Gina rose through the corporate ranks until she became Chairperson of the Hancock Prospecting Company, by 2006 her estimated wealth was supposedly four billion dollars, which made her Australia's richest woman.

Politically Lang Hancock held strongly conservative views and he gave strong support to Queensland Premier Sir Joh Bjelke Petersen and other leading Liberal and National politicians. Hancock strongly opposed aboriginal land rights and he was a passionate advocate for free enterprise activities. "The best government is the least government," became a favourite catch cry of his. Hancock also believed WA should separate from the other states. In fact, during the 1970s, he unsuccessfully bankrolled a secessionist party in the West.

After his wife Hope died, Lang Hancock hired a Philippino woman as his maid. Her name was Rose Lacson. Rose was visiting Australia on a three month visa when the couple became romantically involved, and, despite the huge difference in age, they married on 6th July 1985. It was the third marriage for both partners.

The marriage infuriated Rinehart, who expected to be her father's sole beneficiary before Rose appeared on the scene. After Hancock purchased valuable properties for his new love in Sydney, Gina claimed that Rose was a promiscuous "gold digger". Hancock's only child did not attend her father's wedding. He funded the construction of an ostentatious 16 block mansion named "Prix d'Amour", which overlooked the Swan River. The huge home was supposedly modelled on the Tara Plantation homestead from the famous movie *Gone with the Wind*. At the opulent residence, Lang and Rose Hancock hosted many extravagant high society parties.

Despite numerous quarrels, the couple were still together when the 83-year-old Lang Hancock died from heart failure in 1992. Only three months after her husband's demise, Rose married William Porteous, who had been a close friend of Lang Hancock. By then Gina was publicly accusing her father's widow of nagging him to his death with her incessant shrill tantrums, about which Rose famously replied, "For anyone else it would be a tantrum; for me it's just raising my voice".

Two successive state coroners refused Gina's demands for an official inquest into the causes of her father's death, but finally her intense lobbying resulted in an inquiry being conducted in 1999. Further sensational developments then interrupted proceedings for three months, after Gina was accused of financing the appearance of witnesses who provided falsified evidence.

When the inquest finally concluded, it was officially found that Lang Hancock had died of natural causes. Gina Rinehart still heads the Hancock Prospecting Company and she was recently named in fourth position on "Australia's Rich List"

THE BUSHMAN WITH "A BUILT-IN COMPASS"

Bernard O' Reilly

On 19th February 1937, flying conditions were appalling in the area south of Brisbane. A slow moving tropical cyclone had produced gale force winds, which reached speeds of up to 80 miles per hour and visibility was close to zero.

It was therefore surprising that a VH-UHH Stinson tri-motor aeroplane began its scheduled flight from Brisbane to Sydney via Lismore. The eight-seater plane had five passengers on board and was flown by a very experienced pilot Captain Rex Boyden.

One of the passangers was Joe Binstead, who registered his name as "Barnett" in pre-flight details, because his wife disapproved of him travelling by aeroplane. John Proud was also on board and so was Jim Westray, an athletic Englishman who had recently arrived in Australia. All three became key figures in the drama that later unfolded.

Onlookers later recalled that the cyclonic weather was at its worst after the Stinson took to the air and that all trace of the aeroplane vanished after it lifted off the runway into thick cloud. Six years earlier, when the ill-fated aircraft "Southern Cloud" came to grief, it was recommended that two way radios be installed to facilitate communication between the flight crew and ground control authorities. However, aviation officials had still not made this a mandatory condition when the Stinson began its flight, so it was impossible to maintain contact with the aeroplane.

A massive search was launched after it failed to arrive in either Lismore or Sydney and there were soon various reports of sightings. Residents from the far flung areas of Nambucca Heads, Coffs Harbour, Kempsey, Taree and around the Hawkesbury River, claimed to have seen the missing aeroplane. All these reports proved to be false. After seven fruitless days of searching, it was generally believed that the Stinson had crashed into the ocean near Sydney and authorities assumed the worst for the six people on board. Bernard O'Reilly, however, did not abandon hope.

He was a member of a resilient family who settled near Lamington National Park in south-east Queensland. It was not far from the McPherson Ranges—an extremely rugged area covered with thick rainforest. At first the O'Reillys managed a dairy farm in this inhospitable terrain, but when this venture proved to be unsuccessful, Bernard, his wife Viola and daughter Rhelma, opened a guest house at Green Mountain.

Bernard O'Reilly followed accounts of the missing Stinson with much interest. He soon believed that the plane may have crashed in dense bushland between Archerfield and Lismore near the formidable McPherson Ranges. Consequently, a week after the plane vanished, he packed enough provisions to last for three days and began to search the area. The almost impenetrable foliage on the steep mountains meant O'Reilly had to abandon his hourse. The accomplished bushman then continued on foot, before spending the first night of his search in the unnerving darkness of the jungle.

Around 8am the next day the thick mist suddenly lifted and on the third ridge of the Lamington Plateau, O'Reilly noticed one tree that appeared to have been recently damaged by fire.

Another five hours of hard slogging brought him to within five kilometres of the plateau, and it was there that O'Reilly heard a coo-ee echo across a gorge. Approximately three hours later, when he eventually reached the plateau, mutual coo-ees were exchanged. Before long the rescuer stumbled across two seriously injured men.

Joe Binsead was one of the survivors. It later emerged that he had been knocked unconscious when the plane plummeted heavily into the forest. Fortunately he recovered in time to escape from the smoke filled wreckage with a badly injured John Proud, before the plane became engulfed by flames. Despite the grave dangers they faced, the brave duo assisted a badly burnt Jim Westray out of the plane before it was reduced to charred metal only 30 minutes later. The pilot and two passengers perished in the crash, and soon after nearby trees were also set alight by the intensity of the flames.

Westray, despite his complete lack of bushcraft experience, elected to leave the crash scene to find help. This left the injured Binstead to care for the seriously ill Proud. At first Binstead managed to walk to a nearby water supply, but before long he was only able to crawl through the thorny foliage to obtain small amounts of the precious fluid for himself and his fast fading comrade.

Proud was allegedly scratching a final message on a piece of metal debris when O'Reilly discovered them. Proud and Binstead were ecstatic about being found at last. "We will be able to have that drink at the Australia (Hotel) after all," rejoiced one. "What's the score?" asked the other. (O'Reilly was able to report that Don Bradman was 165 not out in the Test cricket match that was currently being played).

Despite joining in the good natured banter, O'Reilly was daunted by the enormous responsibilities he faced. Proud, with his fractured leg rapidly becoming badly infected, urgently required medical attention, and it seemed only a miracle would save the men's lives. Nevertheless, the determined rescuer was not about to give up. He left the two survivors with cups of tea and food, before departing around 4.30pm in search of help from the nearby settlements of Hillview and Lamington.

On his way, O'Reilly came upon a grim discovery—the body of Westray who had fallen to his death from one of the steep cliffs. O'Reilly later described his long desperate dash down the almost precipitous slopes as "hell driven", but three hours later, after running for approximately 13 kilometres, the exhausted hero stumbled across a young farmer who was out spotlighting.

"I've found the missing aeroplane," O'Reilly gasped, "and there are two men still alive."

A search party was quickly organised. Many local volunteers began to cut out a track through 22 kilometres of jungle foliage and received unexpected assistance from Charles Burgess, "the hermit of Lamington". This local identity had lived alone in the thick bush for some time, after being traumatised by his terrible war experiences, and was able to guide the rescuers along the most suitable routes. By 1.30am two rescue teams were assembled at a designated starting point and the rescue mission began when dawn broke.

A doctor was included in the first group, which began the climb up the steep mountain to the crash site. Behind them another team began to cut a track wide enough to accommodate stretchers. The mission was successful, and by early next day Binstead and Proud were carried on stretchers to the safety of a waiting ambulance. Both subsequently made full recoveries in hospital.

Throughout the ordeal, Proud's festering wounds had

worried O'Reilly, but the maggots, which buzzing flies deposited in the man's wounds, actually proved to be lifesavers. These parasites fed from the gangrenous flesh and halted the spread of infection throughout the helpless victim's body.

Bernard O'Reilly became affectionately known as "the bushman with a built in compass" and he proved to be a modest and self-effacing hero. It seems likely, however, that the scars from his experience left a lasting impression His married daughter, Rhelma Kenny, revealed in her adult years that her father became permanently haunted by his vivid memories of the crash site.

O'Reilly later suggested that aviation officials at airports be given the authority to "ground" aircraft when weather conditions became too dangerous, and this has become an accepted practice in the modern world. O'Reilly was injured during World War 11 conflicts in New Guinea, after previously serving with allied cause in North Africa.

Bernard O'Reilly was 72 years of age when he passed away in 1975.

The wreckage of the Stinson crash

FROM THE STOLEN GENERATION

Harry Penrith claims to have been born under a gum tree at Mosquito Point on the edge of the Wallaga Lake Aboriginal Reserve. The birth took place in a one room corrugated iron house, which was constructed by his father Charles Penrith. The 22-year-old mother, Lily, already had two other children, and she had lost another at birth.

The new baby was immediately placed under the care of Aunt Ruby at the nearby mission, and three months later all three Penrith children were moved to the United Aboriginal Mission's Infants Home at Bomaderry near Nowra on the NSW south coast. Harry Penrith and his siblings became part of a large group of indigenous Australians, who were called the stolen generation.

Before he reached the age of one, Harry became permanently separated from his extended family. He gained no traditional education from his grandfather, who lived until the age of 107. He also soon lost contact with his brother and sister, and in future years Harry only saw his sister twice. The second and final meeting was when he attended her funeral, after she was stabbed to death by an unidentified white man.

The main purpose of the mission was to provide shelter, food and clothing for the children under their care, and to facilitate domestic service training to equip them for their predictable roles in white society residences. Mission visits from the children's families were forbidden.

Harry later walked nearly five miles to attend the nearest public school, where he performed well. However, at the age of ten, he was unexpectedly removed from his familiar environment and relocated at Kinchella Boy's Home near the central coast town of Kempsey. Despite alleged instances of cruelty from one sadistic male teacher, Harry Penrith continued his impressive school performances.

He was encouraged to continue his education at Kempsey High School, where he excelled at cricket football, athletics and swimming. After being elected captain of the Kinchella Boy's Home in 1952, Harry Penrith was given permission to proceed to his fourth year of secondary education, so that he could sit for the Leaving Certificate examinations in 1954. In that year he was inducted as a school prefect, he gained a Bronze Medallion from a local surf life saving club, and his teammates elected him captain of the Smithtown Under 18 Rugby Union team.

Despite his popularity and success, Harry Penrith began to be troubled by attitudes of racism in his community. The Kempsey Swimming Pool was only available to aboriginal customers on one designated day each week, and admittance to the local cinema was allowed once a year. In the town hospital, aboriginal patients were segregated from white patients.

Harry Penrith passed his Leaving Certificate exams and gained employment as a public servant with the NSW Department of Agriculture. During those years, he was accommodated at the Petersham Baptist Young Men's Hostel and on Saturdays he performed outstandingly well for the Parramatta Rugby Union team in Sydney's first grade competition.

Penrith's career also blossomed. He became the most senior aboriginal public servant in the state, after accepting the post of Assistant Registrar at the Wagga Agricultural College. By then he had married a fellow aborigine, and his wife, his four children and he lived in a comfortable residential area of the town.

His sporting success continued and in June 1957 Harry Penrith was selected in the Riverina Rugby Union representative team, which played the famous New Zealand All Blacks at the Wagga Cricket Ground. Penrith is still rated as one of the best players who never played for Australia, and accolades continued for him after he switched football codes: in 1963 it was the Tarcutta player Harry Penrith who was awarded the Wayling Medal, for being the Best and Fairest player in the Group 13 Rugby League competition.

At this time Penrith was also becoming more involved in indigenous matters and this half-caste leader began to campaign strongly on issues such as aboriginal citizenship and civil rights. After winning a prize for an essay that he contributed on these topics, Penrith began to advocate strongly for the introduction of aboriginal kindergartens and indigenous ownership of reserves and missions.

In the late 1960s, Penrith left NSW to study law at the University of Tasmania. There, he became heavily involved with a group that advocated the removal of Truganini's remains from the Hobart Museum, so that this last-known Tasmanian aboriginal person, could be reburied in accordance with traditional beliefs. Around the same time, the increasingly militant Penrith was prominent in the establishment of a Tent Embassy in Canberra.

Promotions continued for Harry Penrith in the public service and in 1974 he was appointed as the Executive Officer of the Aboriginal Hostels Association. Indigenous luminaries such as Charles Perkins and Lois O'Donoghue served as Directors of this organisation during Penrith's tenure and in early 1975 he became Deputy General Manager. When the hostel management was absorbed into the Aboriginal and Torres Strait Islander Commission, Penrith continued to be a high profile employee, who travelled extensively around the country promoting its programs.

By then Penrith had become even more passionate about various aboriginal issues. He wanted a National Aboriginal Art Gallery to be established in Canberra. He also sought a Lands Right Treaty, and when he moved to Townsville in 1975, Harry Penrith helped establish an indigenous independent school. Traditional art, music, folklore and legends formed part of the curriculum.

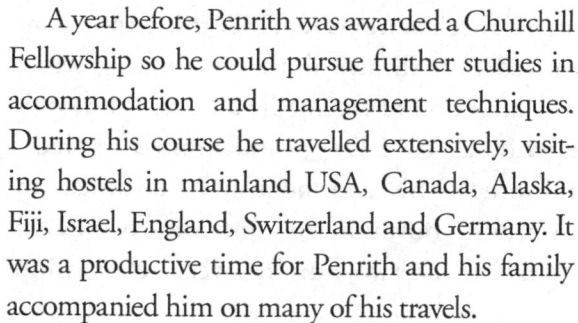

Burnum Burnum

A year before, Penrith was awarded a Churchill Fellowship so he could pursue further studies in accommodation and management techniques. During his course he travelled extensively, visiting hostels in mainland USA, Canada, Alaska, Fiji, Israel, England, Switzerland and Germany. It was a productive time for Penrith and his family accompanied him on many of his travels.

On his return, Harry Penrith began studying for a Bachelor of Arts in Administration degree in Canberra. By then he had re-married, and he had fathered another child, but he was beginning to become more unpredictable in his professional and personal life. A crisis point was reached when Charles Perkins sacked Penrith from the Hostels Association, after he missed a work commitment deadline.

Soon after, Penrith moved to Melbourne, where his second marriage collapsed when he was attempting to cope with alcoholism and a growing gambling addiction. In Melbourne he changed his name to Burnum Burnum, but his reputation among aboriginal leaders continued to plummet.

Around that time, Burnum Burnum unsuccessfully sat for Federal Senate seats on two occasions, but he did gain much acclaim in a new arts initiative he fostered. Burnum Burnum announced himself as a warrior for peace and a public Dreamtime storyteller, which was well suited to his charismatic personality. In this new role he played in three films and wrote a popular book entitled *Burnum Burnum's Aboriginal Australia: A Traveller's Guide*.

During Bicentennial celebrations in 1988, this flamboyant man became involved in a theatrical and symbolic gesture, which captured the attention of the media all over the world. Standing on the white cliffs of Dover and dressed in traditional aboriginal clothes, this enormous man unfurled an Australian flag. Burnum Burnum then grandiosely offered Britain "a fresh start" in its two hundred year relationship with Australia.

His performance in England was largely condemned. Most aboriginal leaders shunned Burnum Burnum, especially when he accepted a consultancy position with their long standing mining company antagonist, Cenzink Riotinto. The salary he received from Riotinto was contemtuously described as "blood money" and his aboriginal advocacy career was ruined.

His health began to deteriorate and a month after he ignored medical advice to have a triple bi-pass operation, Burnum Burnum suffered a massive heart attack. He died on 18th August 1997, at the age of 61.

History may remember this man as being an excellent and articulate communicator, who unfortunately made crucial errors of judgement at critical points in his life.

THE MABO MAN

He was 31 years of age when he learned that his home island did not belong to his aboriginal people. Murray Island was in fact Crown land under the control of the Commonwealth Government of Australia. The revelation shocked Eddie Kocki Mabo and he became a strong and ultimately successful advocate for aboriginal land rights. His original name was Eddie Kocki Sambo. He adopted the name of Mabo to honour his maternal uncle, who raised the lad after he was born on the Torres Strait Island of Mer (also called Murray Island).

Eddie Mabo

Mabo was a 31-year-old gardener at James Cook University in Townsville, when he learned that his home island was not subject to native title. He was shocked to know that Mer did not belong to his Torres Strait Island people who had resided there for decades. Legally the decision came under the statute of "Terra Nullius", which effectively meant that land ownership only began with European settlement. It had never existed for indigenous people.

This long standing Australian law was completely unacceptable to Eddie Mabo, and at a 1981 lands rights conference in Townsville, he provided details about the land inheritance system that had operated in traditional indigenous society. A lawyer in attendance later suggested that Mabo's strong views could form the basis for a lands right test case in the Australian legal system.

On 3rd June 1992, five years after Eddie Mabo died of cancer, the High Court of Australia overturned the legal state of "Terra Nullius". Four judges supported the legitimacy of native title, while three opposed it. From that day native title of land has existed in Australia, and it is the responsibility of the aboriginal and islander people to determine land ownership.

Initially this historic judgement caused emotions to run high. Overnight, vandals desecrated Eddie Mabo's grave, and his body was returned to Murray Island. On the night he was re-buried, respectful local islanders revisited an historical tradition when the ceremony for the death of a king was conducted in honour of Mabo—it was the first time in 80 years that this ceremony had been performed.

In 1992 Eddie Mabo, together with four other recipients, received a post-humus Human Rights Medal. Sixteen years later, the James Cook University Library in Townsville was renamed the Eddie Kocki Mabo Library.

THE FREEDOM RIDER

Charles Perkins was raised by his single parent aboriginal mother in a shanty settlement near Alice Springs. His mother, together with other female members of the Arunta group, was allegedly sexually molested by white men on a regular basis, and her half-caste son Charles was often the target for racial abuse from white students during his schooldays. He did not meet his Irish born father until he was 33 years of age.

Sport was his early salvation. Charlie Perkins became a star soccer player, who played for the famous Everton Club in England. He was later appointed captain-coach of the Pan-Helenic Club in Sydney; the money he earned from soccer helped finance a university course. By then Charlie Perkins was a married man with a young family, and he became the first Australian aboriginal university graduate, after he gained a Bachelor of Arts degree from Sydney University.

Perkins used his qualification to gain employment in the Commonwealth Public Service. By then he had become heavily involved in aboriginal activism and he and his followers embarked on what became known as the "Freedom Ride". This venture involved visiting racially torn NSW towns such as Walgett, Moree and Kempsey, where Perkins publicly revealed discriminations that existed towards black residents in rural communities. At Moree, the activists highlighted the banning of indigenous

Charles Perkins travelling to University, 1963

people from the local public swimming pool, and in Walgett the non-acceptance of aboriginal people in most hotels was publicised.

The abrasive and combative Perkins polarised community opinions. Many applauded him for revealing the apartheid type restrictions that were imposed on aboriginal people in parts of rural Australia. Perkins suddenly obtained a national profile, but conservative figures, such as the future Prime Minister John Howard, criticised him for being involved in political activism, while he was employed as a public servant.

Perkins also publicised the appalling standards of housing and health care that many aboriginal people endured, and he was active in the establishment of a Tent Embassy near the old Parliament House site in Canberra. From this venue Perkins and others activists campaigned for aboriginal land and human rights.

By then Charlie Perkins was battling severe health problems. For years he had suffered from a serious kidney complaint, and his life was in the balance until he fortunately became the recipient of a kidney donation. The operation greatly improved Perkins' health for a further three decades.

Throughout his public life Perkins was constantly at odds with the government of the day. Former Labor Prime Minister Gough Whitlam intervened on his behalf after the Aboriginal Affairs Minister of the day called for Perkins to be sacked. In later years the Hawke Labor Government replaced Charlie Perkins when he was Secretary in the Aboriginal Affairs department. Ironically fellow aborigine Senator Neville Bonner, who was well-known for his conservative views, supported Perkins throughout the furore of an internal investigation. This inquiry later exonerated Perkins from all charges of professional misconduct.

After this bitter dispute, a disillusioned Charlie Perkins returned to his roots around Alice Springs, where local aboriginal law leaders initiated him in Arunta beliefs.

Charlie Perkins, after becoming the country's longest living organ transplant recipient, finally succumbed to kidney failure, and he died in the year 2000 in his 64th year. The controversial activist, who became the most well known indigenous leader and advocate of his time, was afforded a state funeral at Sydney Town Hall, and hundreds of his supporters followed Charlie Perkins' funeral procession through the city.

Over a decade later, on Sunday 24th October 2010, Madeleine Madden, Perkins 13-year-old granddaughter, spoke on every satellite and free to air television station in the country, to an estimated audience of over six million Australians.

Charlie would have been justifiably proud of Madeleine's poised and telling two minute presentation, which called for an end to aboriginal inequality. The young indigenous teenager spoke on behalf of Generation One, an organisation dedicated to building a better future for aboriginal people and placing at least 50,000 indigenous Australians in work by June 2011. Generation One was founded by Andrew Forrest, a leading Western Australian mining magnate.

THE DAPPER SENATOR

At first glance a conservative politician and a "fire talking" aboriginal activist would have little in common, but the childhood years of Neville Bonner and Charlie Perkins were remarkably similar.

Bonner was born on Ukerebagh Island near Tweed Heads on the NSW and Queensland border. His full blood aboriginal mother was forced to deliver her baby in primitive conditions on the island. This deplorable outcome occurred because an after dark government curfew on local indigenous people, prevented her from being admitted to the nearby town hospital to give birth to her child.

Like Charlie Perkins, Bonner had no childhood contact with his father, who returned to England before his half-caste son was born. Bonner was raised by his grandparents, but he did not attend the local Lismore School, because of its segregation policy against aboriginal students. It was not until the family moved to Beaudesert near Queensland's Gold Coast, that Neville Bonner was able to begin his formal education.

After leaving school, Bonner worked as a labourer, before settling on Palm Island near Townsville. In this community, during the 1940s, Bonner became the Assistant Settlement Overseer. By 1960 he had relocated to Ipswich, where he became Director of the

One People of Australia League, a moderate indigenous rights organisation.

In 1967 Bonner became a Liberal Party member and in 1971 was selected to fill a Commonwealth Senate position vacated by Dame Isabelle Rankin. Bonner was then elected to the Senate in his own right in 1972, 1974, 1975 and 1980.

After Senator Bonner criticised his own state branch over contentious indigenous issues, he was dropped from the Liberal Senate ticket for the 1983 Federal elections. Bonner did contest the position as an independent candidate, but narrowly missed gaining another term in Federal Parliament. Later the victorious Hawke Labor government appointed Neville Bonner to the ABC Board of Directors.

Bonner, a softly spoken, articulate and always impeccably dressed man, was mostly very conservative in his political views, but he crossed the floor in Parliament at times to vote against his party's policies on aboriginal welfare issues. In 1979 he jointly shared the Australian of the Year award with popular environmentalist Harry Butler, and in 1984 he gained an Order of Australia, (OA) award. Today a Canberra suburb and a Queensland Federal electorate both carry the name of Bonner.

He was 77 when he died in 1999.

THE AUSTRALIAN OF THE YEAR

Mick Dodson

Professor Michael "Mick" Dodson was born in the NT town of Katherine. After his parents died, Mick Dodson was educated at Monivae College in the western Victorian town of Hamilton. In 1974 Mick Dodson created history, when he became the first indigenous Australian to graduate in a Law Faculty.

Since his Monash University student days, he has become nationally and internationally famous for his prominent advocacy for aboriginal land rights and other indigenous issues. He has also addressed United Nations forums about the rights of indigenous people. Major details in Dodson's curriculum vitae are indeed impressive.

Professor Dodson has been Director of the Australian National University's Centre of Indigenous Studies, and Chairman of the Australian Institute of Aboriginal and Torres Strait Island Studies. Between 1993 and 1998 he served as the inaugural Social Justice Commissioner with the Human Rights and Equal Opportunities Commission.

Previously, between 1976 and 1981, Professor Dodson worked with the Victorian Aboriginal Legal Service. Then, from 1998 until 1990, he was a Counsel assisting a Royal Commission, on the Aboriginal Deaths in Custody issue.

Mick Dodson is a proud and humble man,

who describes himself as being "a persistent buggar". He is a strong supporter for reconciliation between white and black Australians, through better education and an inclusive dialogue. Dodson is always keen to honour aboriginal successes, but he also expects them to be accountable for any failures.

Professor Dodson was named as an Australian Living Treasure in 2003, and in 2008 he was named Australian of the Year. The citation accompanying the prestigious award stated that Mick Dodson was, "A courageous fighter for reconciliation, and for closing the gap between indigenous and non-indigenous Australians".

His brother, Patrick Dodson, is also a noted aboriginal leader.

CHAPTER SEVEN:

OUTBACK WRITERS, SINGERS, ARTISTS AND ACTORS

The earliest written examples from the first settlement era were mostly adaptations from familiar English folk songs and poems. However, those who had been educated in the classical English tradition, tended to create literature that echoed the European environment rather than the Australian scenery, in the images they used. A typical example of this writing style is shown in this extract from William Charles Wentworth's poem, "From Australasia".

William Charles Wentworth

"To those rich pastures,
where the wild herd strays,
The crowded homestead lines the winding stream
On either side, and many a plodding team
With shining ploughshare,
turns the neigh'b'ring soil
Which crowns with double crop the
lab'rers's toil."

In this poem, Wentworth appears to be in a state of denial about the true nature of a typically Australian landscape. In much the same era, a more famous and recognisably Australian poet in Henry Kendall, exhibited similar attitudes, in his lyrical and rhythmical poem titled "Bellbirds".

> "The silver-voiced bellbird, the darling of daytime,
> They sing in September their songs of the May-time;
> When shadows wax strong, and the thunder bolts hurtle,
> They hide with their fear in the leaves of the myrtle."

The poem resonates more in its tone with the dappled woods of England, than with images of the harsh Australian bush. In this particular stanza, Kendall almost apologises for an Australian spring beginning in September, rather than in the May of an English spring.

Perhaps the most substantial first generation Australian poet was Charles Harpur, whose parents were convicts. Harpur was born in 1813, and his Windsor home was surrounded by spectacular Hawkesbury River and Blue Mountains scenery. Consequently his poetry often celebrates the sounds and sights of beautiful natural settings.

Harpur was observant and thoughtful in his writing structure and he combined precise descriptions of the Australian countryside with discerning reflections about man's relationship with nature. The following extract from "Bushfire Part I" demonstrates the powerful imagery that Harpur used to describe an awe-inspiring but dangerous inferno.

> "Within the circling forest he beheld
> A vast and billowy belt of writhing fire,
> That shed a wild and lurid splendour up

Against the whitening dawn, come raging on!
Raging and roaring as with ten thousand tongues
That prophesised destruction! On it came!
Devouring with a lapping hungriness
Whatever shrivelled in its scorching breath—
A dreadful Apparition!"

By the 1890s, the *Bulletin* encouraged Australian short story writers to display their talents, and within the pages of that proudly nationalistic publication, a legendary writing talent was introduced to the Australian public.

THE FLAWED GENIUS

Henry Lawson was born at Grenfell NSW on 17th June, 1867. His father was Niels Larson (a restless Norwegian miner who later changed his name to Peter Lawson) while his mother was Louisa Albury Lawson.

Henry's childhood was both unpredictable and unhappy. After following the gold rush to many locations, his parents separated, and the profoundly deaf Henry was ostracised by peer groups at various schools he attended.

After leaving school at the age of 13, Henry Lawson worked as a builder with his father in the Blue Mountains. Three years later he returned to Sydney, where he lived with his authoress mother, where he came under the influence of her many bohemian acquaintances. The lonely teenager became an apprentice coach painter and unsuccessfully studied matriculation subjects at night.

Lawson experienced many employment failures, before Louisa's republican minded friends persuaded him to try writing. Initially his labours produced "A Song of the Republic", which the *Bulletin* published in 1887. In between various odd jobs and frequent drinking binges Lawson also contributed stories to the *Boomerang*.

A turning point occurred in Lawson's life, when the *Bulletin* sent him on a writing assignment to the outback NSW town of Bourke.

There the sensitive young man's writing was profoundly affected by the harshness of life in this drought afflicted area. The sense of despair and isolation, which permeated many lives of those who lived on tracks further out, left a lasting impression on Lawson's future poems and short stories. His often pessimistic attitude about the Australian bush scene was in sharp contrast to the works of Andrew Barton "Banjo" Paterson, a famous contemporary of Lawson's, who mostly presented outback characters in a more heroic style.

In 1896 Henry Lawson married Bertha Brendt. A boy and a girl were born from the union, but the relationship was always volatile. Henry began drinking even more heavily, and, in the hope of rejuvenating his life, he emigrated first to New Zealand and later to London. Neither new location helped restore either his marriage or his desperate financial position.

Lawson believed a move to London would be the salvation of his writing career, and he was bitterly disappointed when the new location became yet another failure. He did produce the later much acclaimed "Joe Wilson and his Mates" during his three years in England, before ill health forced him back to Sydney in 1902.

The downward spiral continued in Henry Lawson's life. He attempted suicide after his wife and children left him, he spent short terms in gaol for failing to meet his financial maintenance requirements and he spent periods of time in mental institutions. Australia's finest short story teller and poet finally became a vagrant, who begged for money around the Circular Quay area of the city.

Some efforts of help were made by Australian institutions. The Commonwealth Literary Fund granted him a pension of one pound a week, but Lawson's alcohol induced ill health continued to worsen. After suffering a cerebral haemorrhage at the

Abbotsford home of Mrs Isabella Bryers (a loyal sponsor) the flawed genius died at the age of 55 on 22nd September 1922. Prime Minister Billy Hughes and State Premier Jack Lang were among the mourners who attended Henry Lawson's state funeral, and the famous Australian writer was laid to rest at Sydney's Waverly Cemetery.

Henry Lawson, whose occasional laconic wit was interspersed with a passionate and deeply humane spirit of egalitarianism, endeared himself to generations of Australians. He remains a legend today and Lawson was featured on the first Australian ten dollar note. His descriptions about the bleakness and loneliness that colours many outback lives, is vividly revealed in the following extract from his classic short story, "The Driver's Wife".

"There is nothing to see…and not a soul to meet. You might walk for twenty miles along this track without being able to fix a point in your mind, unless you are a bushman. This is because of the everlasting sameness of the stunted trees—the monotony which makes a man long to break away and travel as far as trains can go, and sail as far as ships can sail—and further."

THE BANJO MAN

Andrew Barton Paterson was born on 17th February 1864, nearly three years after the birth of Henry Lawson. Paterson's privileged upbringing was a stark contrast to Lawson's dysfunctional childhood.

A. B. Paterson was born on a property near Orange in NSW, and when he was five years of age the family relocated to the Yass area, not far from the main road that linked Sydney and Melbourne. There the young boy frequently observed bullock teams, Cobb and Co coaches, mountain horsemen, polo players and drovers passing nearby. Such experiences permeated his later writing. At the age of ten, Paterson became a boarder at the prestigious Sydney Grammar School, from where he later matriculated. Paterson then became an articled clerk, before qualifying as a solicitor.

In 1885 he began to have his poetry published. "Waltzing Matilda" was written that year, and gained almost immediate popularity. Another favourite, "Clancy of the Overflow", followed in 1888. In that poem Paterson wrote the following memorable stanza, which describes the appeal the outback environment has for "Clancy" and others of his ilk.

> "…he sees the vision splendid of the sunlit plains extended,
> And at night the wondrous glory of the everlasting stars."

Paterson wrote under the pseudonym of "Banjo", which was the name of a favourite racehorse the family owned. During 1890, Banjo Paterson penned his most famous poem, "The Man from Snowy River", which caught the heart of the entire nation. In more recent years, a film was produced about this legendary Australian hero, and it became a huge box office success.

In contrast to the harsh realism that Lawson conveyed in his writings about outback life, Paterson presented mostly jaunty and romanticised accounts, and the general public adored "Clancy of the Overflow", "The Man from Ironbark" and other rural heroes he created. Soon Andrew Barton Paterson was second only to the famous poet Rudyard Kipling, in his popularity among English speaking readers. The versatile and talented young man still found time, however, to devote attention to other pursuits, such journalism, law, horse race riding, army activities and farming.

In 1903 Paterson married Alice Emily Walker from Tenterfield Station. The couple later had two children, Grace and Hugh. Previously, between 1899 and 1902, Paterson worked as a war correspondent covering the Boer War for *The Sydney Morning Herald*, and the reports he sent back from South Africa received much acclaim. He also covered China's Boxer Rebellion, and during World War I, Paterson served as an ambulance driver with the Australian Volunteers Hospital in France. Prior to the commencement of the Great War, Andrew Barton Paterson was also an editor for a Sydney newspaper and magazine.

The high achiever continued to be successful in virtually every activity he undertook. In 1915 he served as an honorary vet, when he accompanied horses on three voyages to China, Egypt and various parts of Africa. Paterson also turned his attention to sports journalism and during the 1920s he covered First Division Rugby League matches for the *Sydney Sportsman*.

Andrew Barton Banjo Paterson was nearly 76 when he died from a heart attack in Sydney, on 5th February 1941.

SHE LOVED A SUNBURNT COUNTRY

Dorothea Mackellar was allegedly a homesick 19 year old, when she penned the now legendary poem "My Country" in far away London. The start of the second verse still strikes a nationalistic chord with many Australians.

Dorothea Mackellar

"I love a sunburnt country,
a land of sweeping plains,
Of ragged mountain ranges, of droughts
and flooding rains.
I love her far horizons, I love her jewel sea,
Her beauty, and her terror,
The wide brown land for me!"

Isobel Marion Dorothea Mackellar was born into a privileged Sydney family. She became a well-educated woman who spoke several foreign languages and especially enjoyed riding side-saddle on horses at her brothers' properties in the Gunnedah area of north-western NSW.

This prolific writer of short stories and poems never thought of herself as being a true poet. She remained single, though she was engaged to be married on two occasions, and shortly before her death in 1968, Dorothea Mackellar was made an Officer of the Order of the British Empire (OBE). Before she was laid to rest at Sydney's Waverly Cemetery, the poem "Colour" (Mackellar's personal favourite of all the poems she wrote) was read to the large crowd that attended her funeral service. An extract is quoted below.

> *"Great saffron sunset and clouds,*
> *and larkspur mountains,*
> *And fenceless miles of plains.*
> *And hillsides golden-green,*
> *In that unearthly clear shining after rain."*

A draft of Dorothea Mackeller's "My Country"

THE OUTBACK STORY WRITER

Ion Llewellyn "Jack" Idriess was born in Sydney in 1889, but his family frequently relocated around various parts of rural NSW. After contracting typhoid fever as a 16 year old, Ion Idriess almost died, but he recovered his health and started work in Broken Hill, in the assay office of a major mining company. He then worked on a paddle steamer that operated between Sydney and Newcastle and later gained employment as a rabbit exterminator, a boundary rider and a drover. During these eventful times, Idriess travelled frequently with local aborigines in the Cape York Peninsula area.

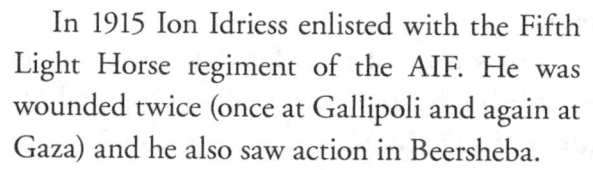

In 1915 Ion Idriess enlisted with the Fifth Light Horse regiment of the AIF. He was wounded twice (once at Gallipoli and again at Gaza) and he also saw action in Beersheba.

After being invalided home from the war front, Ion Idriess resumed his itinerant working life. He surveyed and explored parts of Cape York, he travelled with both missionaries and pearlers in the Torres Strait, he searched for gold in New Guinea and he shot buffaloes in the NT.

During a working stint at Lightning Ridge, Jack Idriesss had contributed short articles for the *Bulletin* and in 1927 he produced *Madman's Island*, the first of his 41 published books. He

Ion Idriess

based himself in Sydney, after he elected to become a freelance writer and in 1931 he wrote the best-selling novel *Lasseter's Last Ride*.

Idriess was a prolific writer. Until 1964 he usually averaged a book a year and in both 1932 and 1940 he had three books published. *Flynn of the Inland* (published in 1932) and *Cattle King* (released in 1936) were both reprinted a staggering 40-50 times. The highly motivated writer usually only took a couple of months to produce his best sellers.

Overall Ion Idriess brought a new understanding to many Australians about outback life. His books combined both heroic and optimistic themes and he presented a positive view about the county's economic potential. His yarns about outback identities and characters were well paced and well structured, and they were based on accurate historical and geographical information. His colourful writing became a model for future narratives, by authors such as Frank Clunes and Colin Simpson.

Around 1932, Idriess married Eta Morris and the couple had two daughters. In 1968 he was awarded an OBE and 11 years later Ion Idriess died in Mona Vale at the age of 90.

QUIRKY CHARLEE

The writing talents of the late Charlee Marshall are known to relatively few people, but his fans regard him as being one of the finest bush poets and humorists of the modern Australian era.

Charlee Marshall

He was born in 1932 during the Great Depression and at various times throughout his life, Charlee Marshall worked as a teacher, a night-shift security guard and a farmer around central Queensland. He and his wife Beryl raised a family, and bred Shetland ponies on their small property near Thangool, and Charlee revealed his talent for writing hilarious short stories relatively late in life.

Marshall became a well-known performer at various folk festivals around Australia, where he won many literary contests. In 1993 Charlee Marshall was inducted into the Wall of Fame at Tamworth's Fireside Festival, and he was a regular contributor at the town's famous Country Music Festival, which always attracts large crowds each January. The fine poet and great mate of many people once wrote the following lines, which now seem to be a fitting eulogy for his life.

> "I place no pride in a silver belt
> Or the glory of games gone by;
> For a gambler plays with the cards he's dealt
> And lives 'til it's time to die."

The last six months of Marshall's life were spent in Rockhampton and he finally lost his battle with cancer in 1995.

Some of Marshall's written creations were published in 1988 in a book called *I Couldn't Bowl For Laughin'*. It was a fitting title for Charlee's creation, because he was a keen and talented country cricketer. As a fast bowler, in a series of annual Brisbane Country Week carnivals, Marshall won the bowling aggregate on a number of occasions, and he loved combining his love of cricket with his short story writing skills. "Crocodile Hanrahan" is one of his creations.

"The incident occurred during the season Kunamundra played Massacre Creek in a Far north Queensland cricket final. As the flood-swollen billabong encroached further onto the playing area, Massacre Creek required 34 runs to win with one ball remaining, and everybody knows that is impossible.

O'Rafferty was batting, and he slogged the final delivery of the match high over long on, and into the outer rim of the billabong. Old Jim, the boundary rider, waded into the shallows to retrieve the ball, when he suddenly noticed a strange looking log with scaly bark markings bumping against the floating ball. Jim hastily withdrew, as the batsmen set off for their seventeenth run.

"Fox the ball!, screamed the now worried Kunamundra skipper, "It's only a log." Despite his insistence, wary fieldsmen still held back, as the perspiring batsmen completed their 25th run.

"Leave it to me," declared ringer Hanrahan, a late arrival on the scene. He dashed into the shallows, swooped on the ball, and flung it low and hard into the wicket keeper's gloves.

"HOWZAT?"

"Out," decreed the umpire, and Kunamundra had won the match by just one run! The excited group of sportsmen drank on into the tropical night, and who won the "Warnie" award for the man of the match?

The unanimous choice was Hanrahan, and his old mother was very proud to receive the trophy after the funeral service ended…"

THE BLANASI MYSTERY

David Blanasi was born around 1930 and he became one of the great didgeridoo players of the 20th century. Blanasi was first discovered when he performed solo on the didgeridoo on a Rolf Harris television program, after which he became a renowned international artist. His didgeridoos are still greatly sought after by souvenir hunters.

Blanasi performed extensively both in Australia and overseas and on tour he was often accompanied by fellow aborigines Djoli Laiwanga and the renowned actor-dancer, David Gulpilli. After Laiwanga died, an emotionally shattered David Blanasi retired alone in a remote part of Arnhem Land. In August 2001 the troubled man vanished without trace.

Some spiritualists claim that they have since been in touch with Blanasi's spirit, and his family eventually conducted a funeral service in his memory.

David Blanasi (far left)

THE "POET LAUREATE"

"One of the finest songwriters I have ever heard, Australian or otherwise."
(David Fricke, Rolling Stones Magazine, in reference to Paul Kelly)

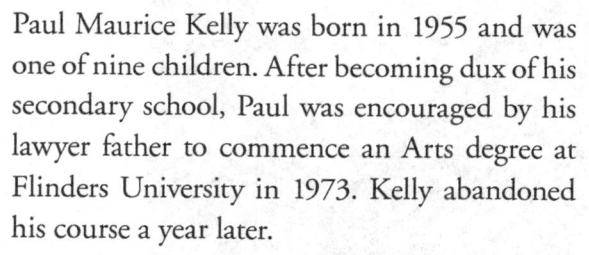

Paul Kelly

Paul Maurice Kelly was born in 1955 and was one of nine children. After becoming dux of his secondary school, Paul was encouraged by his lawyer father to commence an Arts degree at Flinders University in 1973. Kelly abandoned his course a year later.

Paul Kelly's singer-songwriter skills then blossomed and the accomplished guitarist and harmonica player showed his versatility by becoming popular with rock, folk and country music fans. Kelly's lyrics capture the vastness of Australia, both in its culture and its landscape. As a songwriter he has tackled contentious issues such as aboriginal land rights and British nuclear testing and has been described as "Australia's poet laureate".

Some of his most acclaimed compositions include "To Her Door", "Nothing but a Dream", and "Treaty", which he wrote with the predominantly indigenous group, Yothu Yindi. Kelly has encouraged other local musical talents, with both Archie Roach and the late Ruby Hunter benefitting from his support.

Paul Kelly has been twice married and divorced, and he is the father of three children.

His current partner is Sian Prior, who is a university lecturer, accomplished journalist and former opera singer. The couple are presently based in Melbourne.

Paul Kelly

THE RUBY OF ARCHIE'S LIFE

Archie Roach was born in 1956 in the Victorian Goulburn Valley town of Mooroopna, but he was soon rehoused with other indigenous children at the Rumbularah Mission and later at Framlingham, in the south-west of the state. Both his sisters were also forcibly removed from their family and placed by government agencies in orphanages. Archie endured two unpleasant foster home experiences, before finding stability with the Cox family in Melbourne. They loved music, and Archie was given guitar lessons by a daughter of the family.

After his sister informed him by letter about his babyhood abduction, a distraught Archie Roach seised his guitar, a few other possessions and ran away from the Cox family home. For some time he "lived rough" in the streets of both Sydney and Adelaide. It was a period of alcoholism and despair for the troubled young man, but it was also a time when he began to write music. In addition, he met an aboriginal girl called Ruby Hunter, who became his soul-mate, the mother of his children and later his wife.

Ruby Hunter was born near a billabong in the Riverland area of South Australia and forcibly removed from her family by the age of eight. Ruby then lived with a variety of foster parents and was also housed in government institutions.

Hunter was only a teenager when she met Archie Roach at an Adelaide Salvation Army Centre. They soon became inseparable and Roach taught her how to play the guitar and compose songs. Soon she became an accomplished singer, performer and composer in her own right, with "Down City Streets" being an instant hit. Other themes included in her growing repertoire, were songs about women's problems and indigenous issues. Both Roach and Hunter acted in films and the movie titled *The Land of Little Kings*, which focused on the stolen generation, was highly acclaimed.

The original band formed by Roach and Hunter was the Altogethers. Their compositions impressed the legendary Paul Kelly, when the group relocated to Melbourne.

Kelly included them in an opening performance for one of his concerts and in 1990 the song writing and guitar skills of Roach were featured in his first album, *Charcoal Lane*. "Took the Children Away" became an especially popular song. This composition by Roach won two ARIA awards, as well as an International Human Rights Achievement award.

Other albums have followed, and Archie Roach has since been featured in concerts alongside acclaimed international artists such as Bob Dylan, Billy Brag and Suzanne Vega. At times, during his stellar career, Roach has been included among the top 30 artists in the world. He has also presented traditional aborigine stories and he displays impressive strengths and insights in this role.

The spotlight grew dim for Archie when on 17th February 2010 the 54-year-old Ruby Hunter died at their home in south-western Victoria after experiencing heart problems. During their time together, the celebrity couple helped troubled indigenous youths in their Riverland and Victorian homes, and it was a still grieving Archie Roach who returned to live performances at the 2010 Port Fairy Folk Festival.

On the 14h October of the same year, the ARIA award-winning sinnger-songwriter suffered a stroke while conducting song-writing workshops in the Kimberley region. The 54-year-old Archie Roach was transfered to Royal Perth Hospital, where his condition appeared to stabilise.

Archie Roach and Ruby Hunter

YOTHU YINDI

Mandawuy Yunupingu

In the indigenous Yolangu language, Yothu Yindi means "child and mother." The name was adopted by a modern rock band, which had both indigenous and non-indigenous artists in its group. The aboriginal band members originated from an area near Yirrkala, on the Gove Peninsula in Arnhem Land.

The band was founded by bass guitarist Stuart Kellaway. The leader of the group, who provided both vocal renditions and guitar backing, was Mandawuy Yunupingu.

He was born in 1956 at Yirrakala, and is the younger brother of Galarrwuy Yunupingu, whose contributions to the aboriginal land rights movement gained him an Australian of the Year award in 1978. The family surname means "rock which will stand against anything".

In 1988 Mandawuy Yunupingu gained a Bachelor of Arts degree from Deakin University, and two years later he became the first aboriginal School Principal in Australia. During his year of tenure, Yunupingu presided over a curriculum that combined the best aspects of Volngu (aboriginal) and Bolanda (European) educational processes. In 1991 he resigned from his educational leadership position and joined Yothu Yindi as their main songwriter.

Basically the music of Yothu Yindi seeks to combine traditional indigenous music with modern rock and pop songs. The broad aim of the group is to promote mutual respect and understanding between aboriginal and European Australians. This central theme was once summarised by Mandawuy Yunupingu in these words:

> "Racism is a disease in society. We're all equal. I don't care what their colour is, or religion. Just as long as they're human beings, they're my buddies."

Yothu Yindi reached the peak of its success during the 1990s. "Treaty" (written with Paul Kelly) was named as one of the most popular Australian songs of all time and "Djapana" (Tropical Sunset) was also highly acclaimed. In 1992 Mandawuy Yunupingi was named Australian of the Year for his work with the Yothu Yindi Foundation, which was established in 1990 to promote Yulgnu culture and development. The Yothu Yindi band performed live at the Sydney 2000 Olympic Games closing ceremony.

However, despite such heady success, some members of the Yunupingi family have experienced social problems. Mandawuy, who is now a married man and the father of six children, has suffered from chronic alcoholism, which ultimately contributed to advanced renal failure. He has received regular haemodialysis treatment in Darwin and also used traditional healing methods to combat his ill health. Other members of his extended family have faced serious criminal charges for acts of assault.

Outback Stories

Dancers from the Aboriginal band Yothu Yindi

A TALENT THAT DEFIED RACIAL DISCRIMINATION

Albert Namatjira attracted widespread public support for his art work, which has seldom been equalled by any other Australian painter. His amazing ability to capture light at various hours of the day in outback scenery, became hallmarks of his delicate and sophisticated paintings.

Albert Namatjira standing outside Government House, Sydney

Albert (original name Elea) was born on 28th July 1902 at Hermannsburg Mission in the NT, and he was a member of the western group of the Aranda people. After being baptised into the Lutheran faith, Albert Namatjira was removed from his family dwelling and placed in dormitory accommodation at Hermannsburg Mission, from where he attended school.

At the age of 13 the lad returned to his bush domain for six months, and during that time he was initiated in traditional customs. Five years later he left Hermannsburg and married Rubina (formerly Ilkalita) who was a Kukatja woman. The first of their eight children was born soon afterwards, and Albert returned to the mission in 1923.

From Hermannsburg, the young married man worked as a blacksmith, carpenter, stockman and cameleer. Previously, during his boyhood school days, Albert's sketching skills and ability to produce interesting artefacts, had been encouraged by mission administrators. Consequently Namatjira accompanied well-known artists Rex Batterbee and John Gardner, when they journeyed into the interior to paint outback landscape scenes. Batterbee taught their cameleer further painting skills during the two months they worked in the McDonnell Ranges and was impressed with the young aboriginal's artistic potential.

The superintendent of Hermannsburg Mission also noticed the indigenous man's ability and he displayed ten of Namatjira's water colour paintings at a Lutheran conference he attended. Around the same time Batterbee released three other examples of Namatjira's work in Adelaide, and interest began to grow in the emerging artist's landscape paintings.

Soon a solo exhibition of Namatjira's work was displayed in Melbourne. With Batterbee alongside as his mentor, teacher and agent, he began to display a blend of both aboriginal and European influences in his paintings and Namatjira became a national and international artist of renown.

The shy young man suddenly found himself included in the "Who's Who List of Australians" and the recipient of a Queen's Coronation Medal. By then Namatjira was almost a tourist attraction in his own right. However his quiet, dignified public persona was hiding an inner turmoil, as he struggled to adjust to a life of fame in a predominantly European world.

Namatjira also became disenchanted with the attitudes of the Aranda Arts Council, a group, chaired by Batterbee, that was responsible for overseeing both the quantity and quality of the his paintings. Namatjira also encountered disappointing examples of racial discrimination in the wider community. He was ruled ineligible to own property because he had once been a ward of the state. Consequently, he was unable to buy grazing land or own a house in the Alice Springs area. It was rumoured that this recently introduced law resulted from of a dubious conspiracy between local estate agents and landowners, which further disillusioned Namatjira.

By the early 1950s, he left Hermannsburg and lived in a camp on the fringes of Alice Springs. Some appropriate recognition came his way in 1957, when both his wife and he were granted Australian citizenship, but his life was then dogged again by another racially based law.

After Namatjira was found guilty of buying and distributing alcohol to indigenous friends, he was sentenced to six months hard labour in a NT gaol. A huge public outcry about the verdict resulted in the sentence being reduced to three months. However, after serving eight weeks of "open detention" the gifted indigenous artist suffered a heart attack. He died at the age of 57 in the Alice Springs Hospital.

To many, Albert Namatjira remains a brilliant but tragic artist, whose short life was marred by his unsuccessful attempts to exist in two widely different cultures.

Russell Drysdale

THE RED LANDSCAPE ARTIST

Sir George Russell Drysdale relocated to Australia from England at the age of 11. In his early adult years he worked as a jackeroo and the significantly short sighted Drysdale did not take an interest in art until he was in his twenties.

His early years in the art world took him overseas on three occasions, before he started to focus more on the Australian landscape. Soon he began to produce impressive desolate landscapes, which usually contained gaunt figures under threatening skies. In 1944 *The Sydney Morning Herald* commissioned Drysdale to illustrate the effects of a long term drought that had devastated western NSW.

The parched landscape of the NSW outback had a profound effect on Russell Drysdale, and he produced some of his finest art works. "Hills End" was followed by "Sofala", which won the 1947 Wynne Prize for landscape painting. "The Cricketer" followed in 1948 and soon after "The Drover's Wife" was displayed. An admiring public noticed that Drysdale was gradually presenting more redness in his studies of the Australian landscape. Art critic Ron Radford was especially impressed with "The Drover's Wife", enthusing that:

"(it) conveys a sense of desolation, and shows vividly the inhospitable landscape. His dried up earth suggests that man has lost control of the land (but) nature has fought back, and taken back."

Russell Drysdale was knighted in 1969 and in 1980 he was awarded the Companion of the Order of Australia. He died in 1981 at the age of 69 and was pre-deceased by his first wife and son, both of whom committed suicide.

THE NED KELLY ARTIST

Sir Sidney Nolan, the eldest of four children, was born in the inner Melbourne suburb of Carlton in 1919. Nolan left school at the age of 14 and three years later he occasionally attended art classes. Around the same time he became close friends with John and Sunday Reed, who were generous patrons of Australian artists. Albert Tucker, Arthur Boyd and John Percival were included in his group of artistic friends, and they became known as the Heidi group. This commune of artists studied and painted together in the then outer Melbourne suburb of Heidelberg.

Throughout his adult life, Nolan was embroiled in many controversial relationships. He married his first wife Elizabeth in 1938, but their relationship soon ended because of his close involvement with the Reeds. At the time he was openly involved in a sexual relationship with Sunday Reed, but their nine year involvement ended after she refused to leave her husband. Sidney Nolan then married John Reed's sister, Cynthia, and in 1978 he married for a third time. On this occasion the bride was Mary, who was formerly married to John Percival.

Previously Sidney Nolan had deserted from the Australian Army during World War II conflicts, and it was around that time that he became immersed in his iconic Ned Kelly series of paintings. These works left a strong impression on art lovers, who admired the intensity of the colours Nolan used to depict the Australian landscape. The smooth texture associated with the Kelly paintings, heightened the visual impact that the legendary bushranger had on gallery audiences.

Nolan left a series of 27 Kelly paintings at Heidelberg, after allegedly informing Sunday Reed that she could keep as many pieces as she wished. Then, in an apparent change of mind, Nolan declared that all his works must be returned, but Sunday refused to give up 25 examples from the Kelly series. Some observers believe that she may have collaborated with Nolan in the production of the series, which may explain her reluctance to surrender them.

Sir Sidney Nolan later resided in both England and Wales, before he died in 1992 in his 75th year.

Sir Sidney Nolan beneath one of his lyrebird costumes designed for The Australian Ballet, 1987

THE FATHER OF OUTBACK ART

Kevin Charles "Pro" Hart was born in Broken Hill in 1928, and he spent his early years at "Larloona", an outback sheep station 130 kilometres from the famous mining city. During his years with the NSW correspondence school, Hart showed an early aptitude for art and continued his involvement in painting and sculpture after he returned to Broken Hill to work in the mines. He also showed an inventive flair, which led to his commonly used nickname of Pro (a shortening of the word "professor").

At the age of 32, Pro Hart married a 19 year old local woman, and the couple raised five children. Throughout his adult years, Hart frequently expressed his political views. He was vehemently opposed to gun laws, believed that all Labor and Greens politicians should be dumped in the ocean and financially supported Pauline Hanson, the former One Nation leader, in her legal battles.

Pro Hart attracted both praise and criticism for his art. His illustrations of Henry Lawson's poems were generally admired and supporters maintained that Hart captured the true spirit of rural Australia. This respect gained him the title of "the father of outback art". Over the years Pro Hart gained the friendship and respect of various Presidents, Princes and movie stars for his "performance" art. He also appeared in a television advertisement for a carpet company.

Art critics, however, were mostly dismissive about some of Hart's bizarre methods. At times he fired paint out of cannons onto canvas, he dropped paint onto his creations from hot air balloons and produced ice sculptures. Mostly he used the mediums of oil paint and acrylics, but Pro Hart also created many bronze, steel and ceramic sculptures.

In 1976 Hart received an MBE and in 1982 he was the only artist on the continent to receive an Honorary Life Membership from the Society of International Artisque for outstanding artistic achievement. A year later Hart was named an Australian Citizen of the Year.

During the last six months of his life, the advancement of motor neuron disease in his body made it impossible for Pro Hart to continue painting. He died at his home in 2006 at the age of 78. His passing was honoured with a state funeral in Broken Hill. It was the first time such a ceremony had been performed anywhere west of the Blue Mountains region.

Pro Hart, in his studio

THE IMPACT OF INDIGENOUS ACTORS

Robert Tudawali and Ngarla Kunoth had a profound effect on the attitudes of many European Australians after they were plucked from obscurity and became overnight celebrity movie stars in the 1955 film, *Jedda*.

Remote areas of the country were presented meaningfully to city patrons and the strong reliance that white station managers had on their aboriginal support staff was very evident. Some features of *Jedda* were criticised by critics, but the two novice actors received almost unanimous praise.

After his obligations for *Jedda* were completed, Tudawali returned to Darwin to work as a mechanic. By then he had been married for seven years to Peggy, a well-educated fellow aborigine, who initially had a positive impact on Tudawali's life. She encouraged him to become literate in English, but she also passed on tuberculosis to her husband. Their marriage ended after Tudawali became addicted to alcohol. His second marriage failed to improve his illness or his growing drug dependency.

The 38-year-old Tudawali died tragically in July 1967 from horrific burns he received, when he fell into a fire after being involved in a drunken brawl.

Above: Ngarla Kunoth
Bellow: Robert Tudawali

THE "WALKABOUT" DANCER

Tudawali's brief but brilliant acting career was a precursor for David Gulpilil, the indigenous actor-dancer who made a stunning film debut in *Walkabout* during the early 1970s. Gulpilil was born in July 1953 and was raised in a traditional aboriginal environment, where he became a skilled hunter, tracker and tribal dancer. He also attended a mission school at Manigrida in north-east Arnhem Land and added English to the several tribal languages he already spoke.

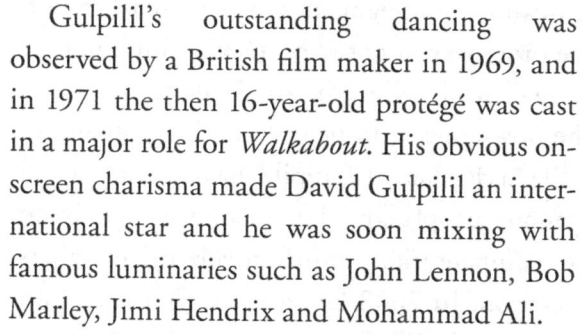

David Gulpilil

Gulpilil's outstanding dancing was observed by a British film maker in 1969, and in 1971 the then 16-year-old protégé was cast in a major role for *Walkabout*. His obvious on-screen charisma made David Gulpilil an international star and he was soon mixing with famous luminaries such as John Lennon, Bob Marley, Jimi Hendrix and Mohammad Ali.

Success in his acting career continued. After *Walkabout* Gulpilil co-starred in the film *Mad Dan Morgan* in 1976 and in that same year he received much acclaim for his role as Fingerbone Bill in *Storm Boy*. Between the late 1970s and the early years of the 21st century, further box office triumphs followed for David Gulpilil in *The Last Wave* (1977), *Crocodile Dundee* (1986), *Dark Age* (1987), *Until the End of the World* (1991), *Dead Heart*

(1996), *The Tracker* (2002), *Rabbit Proof Fence* (2002) and *Ten Canoes* (2006).

David Gulpilil's superb dancing skills resulted in him winning the prestigious Darwin Australia Day Eisteddfod award on four occasions. This versatile performer also showed that he is an exceptional story teller. Gulpilil wrote the text for two volumes of children's stories the themes of which were based on Yolngu beliefs and revealed the reverence traditional aborigines felt for the land they inherited from the Dreamtime.

Controversy has dogged David Gulpilil's personal life. At times he has been the victim of racial discrimination, he has struggled to deal with depression and alcohol abuse, and he has briefly spent time in gaol for substance abuse offences. In July 2006 he was cleared on a charge of carrying an offensive weapon, and eight months later a 12 month domestic violence order was imposed on David Gulpilil, over alleged incidents against his wife, Miriam Ashley.

Fortunately he now appears to be overcoming destructive elements in his life style. David Gulpilil has recently acted for young indigenous people and he became a prominent spokesperson for compensation claims involving members of the stolen generation. In 2008 he returned to acting, and enjoyed a prominent role in Baz Luhmann's blockbuster film, *Australia*. Currently David Gulpilil lives as a respected elder in Ramingining, a central Arnhem Land town with less than a thousand people.

His son, Jamie Gulpilil, who has lived at Ramingining since his birth, has also enjoyed acting success. As a lad he often accompanied David to various film sets and Jamie made his film debut in 2006, alongside his famous father, in *Ten Canoes*.

CHAPTER EIGHT:
OUTBACK TRAGEDIES

CROCODILE ATTACKS

Australia's largest predator is the salt water crocodile. They have existed for approximately two hundred million years and love the creeks, billabongs and coastal waters of northern Australia. The water is their natural habitat and in this familiar environment these reptiles are potential strong, stealthy and silent killers. Crocodiles usually drown their victims, before dragging them to some reedy hideaway, where they are likely to feast on rotting flesh for days.

In the Northern Territory, crocodiles are a significant tourist attraction, and there are more salt water crocodiles in Australia than any other country. The population has now grown to around one hundred thousand.

Charlene O'Sullivan is the mother of 11-year-old Briony Goodsell, who lost her life in a crocodile attack when she was swimming in Blackwater Swamp on 17th March 2009. Ms O'Sullivan joined the growing number of critics of government policy, which helped swell crocodile numbers enormously in recent years.

Shortly before a coronial inquest into her daughter's tragic death near Darwin, Ms O'Sullivan stated that the NT government's wish to expand the salt water crocodile population had increased danger to public safety. More fear was triggered among Territorians in October 2009, after a 4.7 metre monster was sighted, less than a kilometre from where Briony Goodsell was last seen alive. However, it is still surprising that there are only one or two deaths each year from crocodile attacks in Australia. In parts of Africa and Papua New Guinea hundreds are killed by these reptiles each year.

Ignorance about the dangers of crocodile infested waters often leads to disastrous consequences. This may explain why a significant proportion of victims are tourists from other countries. The major blame, however, for a 2002 crocodile death of a foreign visitor in the NT, lay clearly with the victim's Australian guide.

A hungry salt water croc in the Adelaide River south of Darwin.
Briony Goodsell, killed while swimming (inset)

DUTY OF CARE NEGLECTED

The fatality occurred in Kakadu National Park on 23rd October 2002.

Glen Robless was the tour guide. He was well regarded, and had the benefit of 13 years experience. The victim of his irresponsible behaviour was Isabel von Jordan, a 23-year-old German woman, who had recently completed an interior design course. Isabel, and her 21-year-old sister, were enjoying a three month overseas holiday.

Isabel von Jordon

The two sisters commenced their vacation in Indonesia and were in Bali when 202 lives were lost in two horrific bomb attacks launched by terrorists. After this terrifying ordeal, the two young women continued onto Darwin, where they visited friends who had been injured in the bombings, before travelling to some famous tourist spots.

With their Kakadu tour group, they arrived in the late afternoon at Sandy Creek Billabong, 35 kilometres south of Jabiru. There the guide, Glen Robless, observed signs that he believed minimised the danger of crocodile attacks. On the ground were many empty mussel shells, which convinced him that local indigenous women had recently waded safely into the water to collect shellfish. Furthermore, as the sun went down, the light of his torch detected no eyes shining in the darkening water.

One cautious tourist enquired whether it was safe to swim in that area. Robless responded by jumping exuberantly into the water and most of the group joined him. One exception was British tourist Andrew Waters, who stayed on the bank to practise playing his didgeridoo.

Glen Robless, who had not heeded nearby signage that clearly warned about the prevalence of crocodiles in the area, soon returned to shore to persuade others to join in the water fun. It was then that tragedy struck.

A couple of swimmers felt something bump against them. James Rothwell thought that it was a friend playing a prank, but seconds later a scream rang out. At first confused members of the group believed it was a poor taste joke, but when one scrambled frantically to shore the rest quickly followed. A group count then revealed dreaded news—one of the members was missing.

Torches were turned on again and the horrified tourists observed two red eyes glittering in the water near where one of the German women had last been seen. A satellite phone call alerted the Jabiru police and a daybreak search soon revealed a gruesome sight, only two kilometres from where the 23 year old originally disappeared. As a monstrous 4.6 metre crocodile swam under the police boat, the dead body of Isabel von Jordan was clasped in its jaws. Two of the giant reptiles made retrieval of the body a difficult task, but finally their grizzly mission was successful.

Glen Robless was charged with committing a dangerous act causing death and received a three-year suspended gaol sentence. An inquest later showed that drowning caused Isabel von Jordan's death.

THE FRIEND WHO DID NOT RETURN

On the Sunday before Christmas in 2003, three close male friends were enjoying themselves quad riding near the Finniss River, 80 kilometres south-west of Darwin. Shaun Bowers and Ashley McGough were both aged 19 at the time and were accompanied by their close friend, 22-year-old Brett Mann. Brett was a diesel mechanic, who had won the NT Third Year Apprentice of the Year award in 2002.

After the ride finished, the three mud covered mates went to the river bank to wash. However, when they were boisterously splashing each other, part of the bank gave way. Brett Mann lost his footing and fell into the strong current, which swept him away.

Both Brett's friends jumped in to rescue him, unaware that danger lurked nearby. They reached Brett and were helping him up the bank when a huge salt water crocodile suddenly burst out of the rushes. It seised Brett by the shoulder and dragged him under the water.

His two friends swam to a nearby island 50 metres from the bank and clambered up a tree. There the shocked pair clung for safety. At first there was no sign of either Brett or the predator, but about two minutes later the crocodile surfaced with Brett Mann's body in its jaws. The killer tauntingly repeated this act several times, while Bowers and McGough continued to cling desperately to the tree.

They remained all night in their perilous safe haven, and were aware that the crocodile was biding its time close by. Both young men were conscious of the need to keep themselves awake, so that they would not fall out of the tree into the water. The stand off continued as dawn broke, and driving rain and strong winds made survival in their high perch increasingly difficult.

Meanwhile, the NT Tactical Response Group had been searching for the missing trio in their rescue helicopter. Around 3pm (approximately 22 hours after Shaun and Ashley first climbed to safety) the exhausted survivors were spotted. A rescue team in a lifeboat persuaded them to climb down and the finally safe duo were treated for shock and hypothermia at Darwin Hospital.

The victim's body was never recovered. At the 2004 Darwin City Muster, popular country music performer, Lee Kernaghan, dedicated his performance to the memory of Brett Mann.

Ashley McGough and Shaun Blowers

GRANDMA TO THE RESCUE

Bill and Alicia Sorohan had enjoyed camping holidays for many years at Bathurst Bay, 250 kilometres north of Cooktown.

For their 2004 trip, they were accompanied by their son Jason, their daughter Melinda, her husband Wayne, and their friends Andrew and Diane Kerr. Their two grandchildren—six-year-old Kaitlyn and three-year-old Rhiannon were also present, and the Kerrs brought their three-month old baby boy, Kelly.

The group set up camp about 20 metres from the water, but around 4am a massive 4.2 metre salt water crocodile emerged from the bay. The dangerous predator elected to target one of the tents further back from the water, where the Kerr family was sleeping.

A heavy thud outside the tent woke Diane Kerr, and when she peered through the netting she saw the crocodile's gleaming yellow eyes staring at her. She shouted a warning, but the huge reptile burst through the tent flaps, sank its teeth into Andrew's leg and began pulling him out of the tent.

"Get the baby!" yelled Andrew, as the crocodile dragged him further away. Diane plucked up little Kelly with one hand and tried to hang onto her husband with the other, while she continued to scream for help.

Alicia Sorohan was first on the scene and a

Alicia Sorohan with the jaws of the crocodile she tackled

hysterical Diane told her what happened. Alicia rushed out of the tent, and instinctively jumped on the crocodile's back in an effort to distract it from the intended victim. The angered beast broke Alicia's nose, when it abruptly threw back its head and then sank its teeth into the 60-year-old grandmother's arm. Fortunately her 33-year son, Jason then jumped on the reptile from behind and killed the savage predator by firing two shots into the back of its head from his revolver.

Serious injuries were sustained in the brutal attack. Alicia's arm was almost completely severed from her body and her nose was badly broken. Thirty-four-year-old Andrew Kerr sustained a broken arm, a badly broken leg and numerous cuts and bruises.

After enduring a long, painful trip to the Cairns Hospital, Alicia spent two weeks recuperating. Following her release, she still required several months of physiotherapy treatment. The brave Brisbane grandmother was modest about her brave act and fully intended to return to Bathurst Bay with her family for future holidays.

DINGO DANGER

Prior to the infamous Lindy Chamberlain case in 1980, there were no reported instances of dingo attacks on humans. Information about the Chamberlain case is included in the following chapter, but in recent times there have other disturbing examples of dingo attacks in Australia.

Most confrontational incidents have occurred on Fraser Island off Central Queensland, where the influx of many tourists has partly negated fears local animals once held for humans. Some visitors unfortunately feed the Fraser Island dingoes, which encourages the animals to become even more aggressive.

On 4th April 1998 a 14-month-old toddler named Kasey Rowles survived a dingo attack on Fraser Island. In the same location six years later, one-year-old Scarlett Corkel also lived after being attacked by this carnivorous native animal. Jennifer Glandberger, a two-year-old Norwegian girl, was then the target of a non-fatal Fraser Island dingo attack, but three-year-old Clinton Gage was not as fortunate.

On 2nd May 2001, Clinton Gage was attacked at the Waddy Point Camp Ground, which is the same location where Kasey Rowles was previously mauled. Clinton and a young friend set out to explore the nearby sand dunes around 8.50am, when they became aware that dingoes were stalking them. In their panic the children ran towards the dunes, rather than the safety of their campground homes.

Unfortunately the fleeing Clinton tripped and the dingo pack viciously attacked him. After his friend doubled back, and gained help from camp ground residents, Clinton's father, Ross Gage, and his older brother Dylan, rushed to the scene, where they found the victim had sustained serious injuries. His main arteries had been severed in the fierce assault.

At the accident site, a dingo then leapt at four-year-old Dylan Gage and knocked him over. Tragically, after Ross kicked the dingo away and was comforting Dylan, another dingo launched a final fatal attack on the seriously injured Clinton.

The grieving father then carried both his live four year old and his dead three-year-old son, back to the campground, while the stalking dingo pack followed their every move.

DEATH OF AN AUSTRALIAN ICON

Steve Irwin was a larger than life character—a crazy risk taker who appeared to be permanently hyperactive. His life was devoted to preserving natural environments and educating people about Australia's unique animal life.

Steve Irwin

The trappings associated with his celebrity status held little relevance for this typically "Aussie" bloke. Irwin once famously declined an invitation to have dinner with ex-American President Bill Clinton, because "it was not his thing". Such quirkiness only added to his popularity, and Steve Irwin became a much loved celebrity, especially in America and Australia.

Many of Irwin's actions were outrageous. He once advanced on all fours towards a pride of lions in Africa and when he called out "hey" the big cats ran away. In one high risk encounter, at an Alice Springs stage show, Irwin was bitten by a two metre long Perenti lizard. He also wrestled a large anaconda at the University of California. Then, on the day before he died he swam with a highly venomous two-metre sea snake.

Irwin polarised public opinion. To many, he was a national and international hero and a great ambassador for his country. Others regarded him as being an embarrassing "ocker", whose risky antics crossed the line. In one much publicised incident, Irwin received widespread criticism, after he held his one-month-old son close to the mouth of a crocodile. However, this gregarious man was very generous with both his time and money. Much of his earnings from his promotional activities and his Sunshine Coast Zoo, were ploughed back into animal conservation and welfare projects.

Given his devil-may-care attitude, Steve Irwin's sudden and bizarre death was almost predictable. He was, however, desperately unlucky, as the number of deaths from stingray attacks is extremely minimal. A Melbourne man died in 1945 after being lashed with a ray's barbed, whip-like tail. Forty-three years later, a man named Jeff Zahmel suddenly passed away, after an unfortunate encounter with a sting ray. Rays are mostly not aggressive and seek to avoid contact.

On 4th September 2006, at Batt Reef off Port Douglas, Steve Irwin was working on a north Queensland film documentary titled *Ocean's Deadliest*. The segment being filmed was to be included in a series of 26 programs for an American Cable Television company. During a break, Irwin decided to obtain extra footage for his daughter Bindi's upcoming TV program. For one photographic image he swam alongside a bull ray that was swimming in shallow water.

When he swam over the top of the ray, it went into defensive mode and made an upward swipe with its tail. The sharp barbs ripped Steve Irwin's chest open and penetrated close to his heart. Irwin frantically pulled at the barbs, which had slashed through his ribs, and left the gaping wound near his heart. Blood then poured into the water, before members of the film crew could reach the pain stricken victim.

A distress call was transmitted at 11.21am, while desperate attempts were being made to revive him. Emergency Management personnel were at the accident scene within 30 minutes, but nothing could be done to save Steve Irwin's life. Basically, the horrific wound inflicted was the equivalent of having a large knife thrust deeply into his chest.

News of his death quickly flooded the world media, and his American wife, Terri, and his two young children, rushed back to north Queensland from their Tasmanian hiking holiday. The gates at Australia Zoo on the Sunshine Coast became a shrine that was soon covered with stuffed toys, candles, flowers and children's drawings. Many people left poignant messages on Steve Irwin souvenir T-shirts and large crowds later flocked to his funeral, which was screened live on television, both in Australia and the United States.

Terri Irwin with Bindi and Bob at the memorial service for Steve, 2006

Tracks Further Out

DEATHS IN THE OUTBACK

Approximately 40 people lose their lives from road deaths or dehydration each year in the Australian outback. Once travellers leave the comforts of civilized life for tracks further out, they are often confronted by unfamiliar perils. A burning question often surfaces—how does one survive when the temperature soars to 45°C in the shade and you are hundreds of kilometres from the nearest person?

Four common sense precautions can reduce the dangers newcomers face: carry enough water, inform others about the expected duration of your trip, have a thorough knowledge of the vehicle you are driving and remain close to your vehicle while waiting for help to arrive.

However, when common sense vanishes in the isolated outback, and reckless ignorance takes over, results can be fatal.

Remote desert settlement, NT

A DEATH WHICH LED TO FREEDOM

Uluru, often known as Ayers Rock, has unfortunately featured in many outback accidents. At least 35 people have died from heart attacks after attempting the strenuous climb to the summit. There are also numerous instances of serious injury, and even death, when visitors accidentally fall from steep parts of the giant monolith. One fatal casualty was David Brett. A bizarre but very positive outcome, finally resulted from his unfortunate demise.

David Brett was motivated by personal and spiritual issues when he made the decision to climb Uluru on Australia Day, 1986. The Englishman had been in Australia for four years, and during that time his interest in elements of spiritualism and the occult had increased his quest for self knowledge. Brett's soul searching lured him to Australia's famous tourist resort, when mid-summer conditions made the challenging climb even more gruelling.

Brett delayed his ascent of Uluru until just before sunset, so fading light prevailed when he commenced climbing the steep and difficult western side of "the Rock". His emotional state prior to the attempted climb has been much debated. Some who knew him believe that he was mentally ill, and that he expected to be transported to heaven from the top of Uluru. His true motivation behind the dangerous attempt may never be known, but the result was tragic—David Brett fell 46-metres to his death from high on the monolith.

His body was not discovered for eight days and by then the remains were both badly decomposed and riddled with dingo hair. The corpse was close to where a search party found clothing belonging to Azaria Chamberlain, who had disappeared six years before. On this occasion another vital discovery came to light, which ultimately overturned a miscarriage of justice.

Close to David Brett's remains, was a baby's knitted matinee jacket. It was later identified by Azaria's mother, Lindy Chamberlain, as being the garment her child wore on the night of 17th August 1980, when the infant was taken from a tent by a dingo. Despite her plea of innocence, Lindy Chamberlain was sentenced to life imprisonment for murder after her baby vanished. Consequently, the discovery of David Brett's body, unexpectedly led to the release of a wrongly convicted woman.

It was an incredible coincidence that David Brett fell to his death near that vital piece of missing evidence in the Chamberlain case, and the chances of this occurring again are now even more unlikely. Today many visitors elect not to scale Uluru. It is a decision that respects the beliefs of many indigenous Australians, who regard the rock as a sacred monument.

Uluru, NT

A FORTUNATE SURVIVAL

"If ignorance is bliss, tis folly to be wise."

William Shakespeare penned this opinion in his famous play *Hamlet*. It seems a very apt quotation for the life threatening situation that Masa Hia Ono inflicted on himself in early January, 1994.

Incredulous members of the search party who subsequently rescued the young man, dubbed him "Japan's Mad Max" and Masa was a great fan of the famous screen character. He emulated his hero when he purchased a 250cc Honda motorbike in Sydney during his holiday in Australia. Masa then blithely decided to ride his cherished new acquisition into Australia's desert country, before returning to Japan.

Consequently, in late 1993, the naive Japanese tourist arrived at the Simpson Desert. There he unknowingly confronted 156,000 square kilometres of red sand and mulga scrub. The Simpson Desert was bound on the northern side by the Great Sandy Desert, while the equally inhospitable landscape of the Great Victorian Desert formed a southern boundary.

The intrepid and blissfully ignorant young man decided to head east towards remote Warburton on the Gun Barrel Highway—a distance of 450 kilometres. For such an arduous trip, Masa only carried an inadequate four litres of water.

Early next day, his bike rack fell off so Masa recklessly dumped most of his vital supplies on the side of the road, before heading towards Carnegie Station. Then his petrol tank ran dry, which abruptly ended his journey, as his spare supplies of fuel had been dumped further back on the highway.

Luckily Masa was stranded only ten metres from a water

hole. Some thoughtful past visitor had kindly left a cup nearby for the use of fellow travellers, but Masa left it untouched—he believed it was some kind of radio transmitter! Even under the shade of a nearby tree it was 41°C that day, but for some inexplicable reason the young tourist sat out in the open in 50° heat. By then he had no food and did't drink water from the muddy pool, as he feared it would make him sick.

New Years day 1994 dawned, by then Masa was seriously delirious, sunstruck and dehydrated. Around that time a station worker from Warburton reported him missing and a police search for the missing traveller began. Next day, when the temperature had climbed to 35°C by 8am, the police discovered a totally delirious young man, dressed in shorts, t-shirt and socks, lying on his back in direct sunlight near a dam. His rescuers fed him with dehydration tablets. They could not believe Masa was still alive and forecast he would have died by nightfall, if he had not been found.

Masa Hira Ono's one sensible act in this embarrassing and near fatal chain of events, was to give prior notice at Warburton Station about his travel plans. This strategy finally saved his life. Later Constable Benton from the rescue group accurately summed up the bizarre near-tragedy.

"He could have survived for quite a while with sensible survival steps…it was just stupidity that nearly killed him."

As Shakespeare accurately stated many decades ago: "If ignorance is bliss…"

A FATAL ACT OF FOLLY

She died alone in the burning sands of the South Australian outback. Just prior to her death, she unknowingly walked past water bores, water troughs and a 400 litre water tank, which was then half-full. Her partner survived in the same hostile terrain, because he returned to their four-wheel drive until rescuers arrived.

Gabriele Grossmueler was a 28-year-old Austrian medical student and Karl Goeschka (her boyfriend for 11 years) was a research assistant. Karl and Gabriele had embarked on a whirlwind tour of outback Australia in a hired campervan.

On Monday 7th December 1998, they reached the tiny settlement of William Creek, which boasted a population of 15 people. This extremely remote outpost is in the middle of the Oodnadatta Track on Anna Creek Station in South Australia. Nearby road signage (which included a graphic image of a skull and crossbones) urged travellers to check in at the William Creek Hotel, before continuing on to Lake Eyre.

The young couple heeded this advice. Karl informed the publican's son they would be exploring Halligan Bay Track, before returning by noon next day. The son could not locate the hotel's current Search and Rescue register, so he noted the couple's arrangements in a new book. The Austrian tourists carried good supplies of food and water with them, as well as a survival book. The contents advised all outback travellers not to leave their vehicle if lost or injured and to conserve energy by staying out of direct sunlight.

After arriving at Halligan Bay, where the temperature soared to 40°C in the shade, Karl and Gabriele became hopelessly bogged in sand. They lacked the bush knowledge to dig themselves out of their predicament and feared they could be isolated for weeks, if rescuers did not soon arrive. Hours later, at 4pm on the Wednesday, the desperate couple agreed on a disastrous decision, They would walk back through the stifling heat to the William Creek Hotel.

The weary couple trudged along the corrugated track till late that night, before resting until dawn. By then Karl felt too ill to continue, but Gabriele foolishly soldiered on towards the hotel, while her lover finally found his way back to the stranded vehicle by Friday.

By then the couple had been missing for four days, but authorities were unaware of their desperate situation, because of the irresponsible behaviour of the publican's son. Soon after Karl and Gabriele drove away, he left the hotel for Melbourne, without informing his father about the entry in a new book that detailed the tourist's travel plans. Consequently, no one was aware of the missing traveller's plight and a despairing Karl Goeschka began to lose hope.

Three days later, just over ten kilometres from the William Creek Hotel, Christopher Kuppers and Hans Martin-Kieser, made a grim discovery. The two German tourists found a badly decomposed body with a bottle containing about 1.5 litres of water nearby and a note with the piteous message of "HELP" written in both English and German.

They notified the publican, and he contacted Senior Constable Paul Liersch at the Maree Police Station. Two CIB officers from Coober Pedy joined the rescue crew, who made their way back to Halligan Bay where Karl Goeschka was found in a distressed condition.

Today a white cross stands on Halligan Bay near Armistice Bore, which commemorates the place where Gabriele Grossmueler perished. The publican's son was reprimanded by the coroner for his careless actions, which partly caused this unfortunate death in Australia's outback.

A FREE SPIRIT SURVIVES

Misgivings were first felt about a missing person's welfare after an old blue bicycle was found abandoned on a remote dirt track 50 kilometres south of the Sandfire Roadhouse, in the far north of WA. It was feared the cyclist may be dehydrated, disoriented and even dead and a search party was quickly organised. Identification documents near the bicycle, revealed that the missing person was likely to be a 33-year-old Alaskan man named Robert Bogucki.

The American fire-fighter and adventurer was 200 kilometres from the found bicycle and was blissfully unaware about growing concerns for his safety. It was later revealed that he abandoned his bike because he found it easier to travel on foot, and it was certainly a challenging route that he planned. Bogucki decided to walk 600 kilometres across the arid Great Stony Desert to Fitzroy Crossing—a journey that most experienced Australian bushmen would shun.

After police examined Bogucki's identification documents and personal papers, they contacted his Texan girlfriend, Janet. By then two weeks had elapsed since the search began, but initially she was unconcerned. Janet informed the Australian authorities that Bogucki may have deliberately avoided contact with rescuers, because he was focused on a personal mission, which would challenge his endurance capabilities. He also hoped to discover "spiritual enlightment" in the Australian desert. Amid all the mayhem and confusion, the eccentric Alaskan continued to enjoy his solitary trek through the arid wilderness. However, by then his Californian parents had become concerned, especially after the WA Government abandoned the search for their son.

Bogucki's parents first approached American Government

officials to help locate their missing son. They then elected to offer $40,000 for the services of a special American response unit, which was directed by Garrison St Clair, a retired US Army Lieutenant. Allegedly, part of the hiring fee was spent on custom made leather shoes for three tracker dogs, to protect them from Spinifex thorns in Australia's outback!

Amazingly, after the American visitors departed on a five day search mission, the pampered pooches discovered Bugucki's tracks 223 kilometres south-east of Broome. The good news became even better, as the tracks indicated that the missing man was fit and healthy. Two days later the search party came across a bible, clothing and a water bottle that had all been abandoned in the harsh terrain.

Finally, on Monday 23rd August 1999, a figure was spotted walking inside a deep gorge. After they made contact, Bogucki, who was dressed in a filthy t-shirt and army trousers, allegedly said "I'm done with walking!" It was his first contact with other humans in seven weeks. Bogucki revealed that, shortly before he was discovered, he spelled out the word "HELP" on the ground with large rocks, but his message was not seen.

Inside Bogucki's bag was a clean white shirt, which he intended to wear when he hitch-hiked a ride into Fitzroy Crossing at the end of his trip. He had lost nearly 30 kilograms during the 42 days he had spent alone in the desert, but overall Bogucki was in surprisingly good health, when a Channel Nine helicopter touched down near him.

The intrepid loner tried to avoid the media frenzy that was developing around him and a kindly Broome policeman named Geoff Fuller, made his home available for Bogucki to recuperate in private. Fuller also censored incoming mail that criticised the Alaskan's solitary expedition.

Was such criticism warranted? Much time and money had

been spent before this unusual man was located, but the inconvenience was not directly caused by his actions. In many ways Robert Bogucki was an exemplary traveller in the Australian outback. He ensured that he was physically able to withstand the hardships of his journey and his family knew his travel plans before he embarked on his lone mission.

Overall the bushcraft and survival skills that the American visitor displayed were outstanding. Bogucki dug successfully for water during his long stay in the outback and the holes were then carefully covered, so that native animals would not injure themselves. Rubbish he accumulated was carried with him, rather than being strewn around the desert and he did not seek the help of others for much of his long mission in an Australian desert.

A DREAM BECOMES A NIGHTMARE

Ethel Hethering

Ethel Hethering deserved to fulfil her dream of seeing the Australian outback. The 52-year-old English mother of two had long provided diligent care for her 70-year-old husband, who was afflicted with Multiple Sclerosis (MS). Despite her personal hardships, Ethel Hethering was a constantly cheerful woman and an active social worker in her home community.

Ethel enjoyed the companionship of her cousin and her cousin's husband, on her trip "down under" and on 27th October 2004 (the last night of their memorable holiday together) they shared some farewell drinks at the Outback Pioneer Hotel at the Uluru resort of Yulara. After her friends retired for the night around 9.30pm, Ethel began chatting to some indigenous people from Mutyulu, a NT aboriginal community about 19 kilometres from Uluru.

It is difficult to understand why Ethel Hethering then decided to travel with her aboriginal companions back to Mutyulu. Perhaps she was curious to experience the culture of indigenous people, but for whatever reason the next few hours of her life were spent in their community.

Subsequent decisions were also inexplicable. Ethel left Mutyulu without notifying anyone about her plans; perhaps she was emotionally disturbed by that very different environment. Maybe she believed she might miss her return flight if she relied on others to help her. No one can be sure about the visitor's motives, but the outcome of her decision to return alone to the Hotel became a disaster.

Next day her anxious cousin notified local police when Ethel failed to return. At first a concentrated search found no trace of the missing English woman. Then, 36 hours after Ethel Hethering was last seen at Yulara, her body was discovered on an isolated track named Old Petermanns Road. The obviously disoriented woman had meandered approximately 22 kilometres in her long final walk, but in the opposite direction to where Yulara was located.

For some time authorities debated the exact cause of death. Was her life ended by a combination of circumstances, such as the brutal heat and her complete lack of water? An autopsy did little to clarify the dilemma, but a later coronial inquiry found she had died from hypothermia, which was linked to the very hot conditions she encountered on her fatal walk.

After her death was confirmed, a special memorial concert was held in her home town back in England. At least six hundred pounds was raised and these proceeds were donated to breast cancer research.

CHAPTER NINE:

DISASTERS AND MYSTERIES OF THE OUTBACK

BOMB ATTACKS IN NORTHERN AUSTRALIA

On 19th February 1942, approximately 200 Japanese fighter planes launched a massive bombing blitz on Darwin. It was the most comprehensive World War II bombing attack from the Pacific enemy since the blitzing of Pearl Harbour on 7th December 1941. The bombing of Darwin became the first of many air assaults on Australia's northern borders. The attacks from Japan are currently the only time Australia has come under direct threat from a foreign country.

The assault on the capital of "the top end" was launched from Japanese aircraft carriers in the Timor Sea. Darwin's harbour area, airfields, hospital and the main post office were especially targeted. At least 240 people were killed and 400 injured in the savage 40-minute bombardment; fatality rates among postal workers were especially high. Some observers believed the true casualty rate was even higher, but government authorities altered death rate figures in the interests of public morale.

At the time of the bomb attack, Darwin Harbour was crowded with allied ships and 27 vessels suffered significant damage. Scenes at the main airport were chaotic and close to 80 aeroplanes were damaged beyond repair. Prior to the attacks from the air, many Darwin women and children had been evacuated, but panic broke out among those remaining after the first wave of air attacks was experienced. It is estimated that at least half of Darwin's usual population abandoned the disaster scene, as soon as escape became possible.

Two weeks later the famous WA pearling town of Broome became the target of the nation's second worse air attacks. Seventy residents were killed and at least 40 injured. In other northern Australia attacks, Townsville was bombed on three separate occasions, while Katherine, Derby, Wyndham and Port Hedland were also attacked by Japanese aircraft.

The explosion of an oil storage tank,
Darwin, 19[h] February 1942

EARTHQUAKE AT MECKERING

The number of recorded earthquakes in Australia would surprise many, but overall their damage has been minimal because they usually originate in sparsely populated areas.

A typical example is the 1941 earthquake that occurred in the remote Western Australian town of Meeberrie. The Richter scale reading for that natural disaster was 7.1, which is the highest current reading for any Australian earthquake. However, there were no deaths recorded, and property damage was minimal.

The 1968 earthquake that occurred 130 kilometres east of Perth in the wheat growing area of Meckering, was less severe in intensity, but the effects were far more destructive. Warning signs of the catastrophe actually emerged 11 days before the main quake. Minor tremors occurred and an ancient 60 kilometre long fault line below the earth's surface was re-activated.

Then, on 14th October 1968, the ground opened up when the fault thrust itself upwards, and vertically displaced the ground surface over a 200 kilometre area. Meckering was close to the epicentre of the quake and most of the town was completely destroyed. Miraculously there were no fatalities amidst all the collapsed buildings.

Before long, graphic descriptions about the Meckering earthquake were being circulated. Fellow Australians learned that two distinct ground waves (travelling at an approximate rate of 10 kilometres an hour) had rippled across the main street. Around the town area ground cracks continued to open and a pungent carbine type gas smell enveloped Meckering.

Two metre high bumps suddenly appeared on a road near the town. The occupants of a car luckily avoided having a serious accident that day, after an underground fault line abruptly lowered the normal level of the road by a staggering 1.8 metres.

Aerial view of a railroad crossing surface rupture near Meckering

CYCLONES AROUND AUSTRALIA

Modern Australia's most notorious cyclone, which wreaked havoc on Darwin during Christmas 1974, was not a unique event. Since recorded history, documented examples of often terrifying cyclones have battered mainly northern areas of the country.

The worst cyclone, which produced more fatalities than any other known natural disaster in Australia's history, was Cyclone Mahina, which brought widespread mayhem to the Cape York area in March 1899. Four hundred lives were reportedly lost and approximately half of the dead were either pearl fishermen or local indigenous people.

Life on the water is especially hazardous during cyclones. On 24th December 1875, 69 lives were lost on ships at sea after a dangerous cyclone developed in WA's Exmouth Gulf. Only nine years later the death toll in the West reached 140, when 40 pearl luggers sank beneath the waves during a fierce cyclone near Lagrange, off the far west coast. In March 1923, 20 lives

A home damaged by Cyclone Larry, Moresby Queensland, April 2006

were lost on the steamer "Douglas Mawson" near Groote Eylandt on the Gulf of Carpentaria. Port Hedland suffered 45 fatalities in an 1894 cyclone, and the pearling town of Broome has also recorded huge death tolls from past cyclones. Fifty perished in a fierce 1908 tempest and the number of fatalities exceeded 140 in the 1935 cyclone.

In 1971, residents of the north Queensland city of Townsville, and the nearby resort area of Magnetic Island, reeled from the effects of a huge tropical storm named Cyclone Althea. At the height of the storm winds reached the incredible speed of 196 kilometres per hour, and 90% of homes on Magnetic Island were either extensively damaged or totally destroyed.

Cyclone Larry lashed north Queensland in 2006 and 66 lives were finally lost in this tropical disaster. Previously, on the other side of the vast continent, southern areas of WA were savaged by Cyclone Fifi in 1991; there were 29 fatalities from that catastrophe.

Darwin has always been prone to cyclones. Dangerous storms brought much destruction to the capital of "the top end" in 1878, 1897, 1927 and 1937. However, nothing compared in ferocity to the cyclonic forces that struck this isolated city on Christmas Day, 1974.

A CYCLONE CALLED TRACY

"We could hear roofs being ripped around us as if they were pieces of paper. It was like bombs going off. In minutes our house was blown apart...God knows how we survived."

This graphic eye witness account was provided by a fortunate survivor of Cyclone Tracy, which brought mayhem to Darwin during the height of the 1974 festive season. Prior to the late hours of Christmas Eve, residents were mostly dismissive about the weather warnings that were issued over three successive days. During the past mostly uneventful 37 years, locals had received dire warnings about cyclones, which ultimately passed the city by. Complacent Darwinians were more concerned with organising parties than "battering down the hatches" for yet another cyclone threat.

However, early on Christmas Eve, the weather situation deteriorated rapidly, after Tracy changed direction near Bathurst Island and headed back towards Darwin. By noon a concerned weather bureau issued a Flash Warning Number 16, which indicated that residents could expect highly destructive winds to develop either overnight or early on Christmas Day.

Regular warnings from the bureau continued throughout Christmas Eve and by 2.30am on 25th December, it was predicted that the eye of the storm would pass over the city. Despite the meteorologist's ominous messages, the pubs around Darwin were still crowded with boisterous revellers. The party mood, however, was about to dramatically end.

Ferocious wind gusts, reaching a speed of 200 kilometres per hour, lashed Darwin in the early hours of Christmas Day. The city was plunged into darkness, after electricity supplies failed, but around 4am Cyclone Tracy seemed to have moved on. An eerie quietness hung over the city, as relieved citizens emerged from their shelters to survey the damage from the freak storm, which appeared to have passed. However, after the eye of the storm passed over the city, the winds returned from a different direction with the same destructive ferocity. More lives were lost and many others were injured when the cyclone changed course.

> "It looks as though an atom bomb has hit... There's not a tree with a branch left on it...there is no food, no power and no water." (Darwin ham radio operator, as the full extent of Tracy's carnage became evident)

The next day conditions finally began to moderate and the full extent of the catastrophe became evident to residents. Darwin was virtually destroyed. Many buildings lay in ruins, vast amounts of strewn debris rendered most roads impassable and the airport, where many aircraft lay wrecked on the tarmac, was completely inoperable. One World War II veteran likened the chaotic scene to Hiroshima, after the atom bomb was dropped on that Japanese city.

The final death toll from that Category Four cyclone was 65, and the destruction to buildings was so horrendous that some experts later recommended the entire city be rebuilt. A large percentage of local residents were air-lifted to southern parts of the country, to avoid the risk of disease epidemics.

In the aftermath of Cyclone Tracy Major-General Alan Streeton, the Director-General of the National Disasters Organisation, made contentious accusations about official mismanagement. His criticisms were later rejected by the incumbent Prime Minister, Malcolm Fraser.

Many new structural building changes were advocated for much of Darwin following this major natural disaster and significant alterations were made to emergency response procedures.

Caravan park in Darwin after Cyclone Tracy, 1974

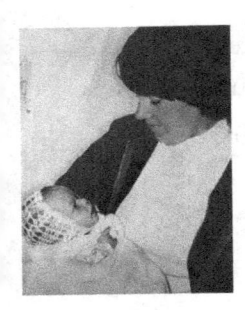

DINGO DEATH AT ULURU

"A dingo took my baby!"

The key figure in a real life drama was Lindy Chamberlain, who became the centre of global media attention on 17th August 1980, after she screamed "A dingo took my baby!" near the popular outback tourist attraction of Uluru. Her husband, Michael Chamberlain, and other nearby occupants of the Ayers Rock (Uluru) National Park Camp Ground all frantically searched in the darkness for the missing ten-month-old Azaria Chamberlain, but to no avail.

The disappearance soon became a criminal case, which ultimately caused an innocent woman to be gaoled for nearly six years. The total cost of investigations, inquests, appeals and compensation claims, exceeded twenty million Australian dollars. Reputations of the NT Government and police force, much of the national media and a previously reputable forensic scientist, were all greatly tarnished.

After Azaria vanished, Derek Roff, the head ranger of the park, advised the baby's parents not to handle anything at the site before the police arrived. This suggestion was supported by Sally Lowe, another camp resident. Ms Lowe felt especially uneasy about the situation. She had already observed what appeared to be blood spots on bedding and clothing,

Above: Lindy Chamberlain holding Azaria, 1980s
Bellow: Lindy and Michael Chamberlain leaving court

Disasters and Mysteries of the Outback

when she supervised Azaria's six-year-old sibling, Aidan, while others searched the nearby area for the missing baby.

Police arrived approximately 30 minutes after being notified. Lindy Chamberlain then informed Constable Frank Morris, that Aidan and she had spotted a large dingo slinking out of the tent where her two youngest children were sleeping. The animal appeared to be dragging a heavy object across the ground, but Lindy couldn't identify what it was, because of poor visibility. She also informed Morris that Azaria was wearing a white matinee jacket at the time of her disappearance.

Lindy Chamberlain described how she shooed the animal away from the tent. She was relieved to find four-year-old Reagan Chamberlain still sleeping safely, but then realised her baby was missing. Later both Michael Chamberlain and Sally Lowe claimed they heard a child cry out in the night, before the shocked mother discovered that her baby had disappeared.

Clockwise, Right to left: the inquest at the site where the incident happened, Lindy Chamberlain and Azaria, the baby's jacket

Murray Haby, a tourist who joined the initial search, found evidence that suggested a dingo had dragged something across the ground towards the camp car park area. Haby's revelation began a series of poor decision making by the police at the crime scene. The parents were not informed about this new development, the area was not cordoned off from the general public and no official photographs were taken. Furthermore, when Constable Morris asked questions of witnesses that night and next morning, no written notes were taken about the alleged chain of events.

By then it became increasingly unlikely that a baby could survive a cold night in the desert, and Constable Morris informed the parents that they needed to sign a "form of release" prior to an inquest being conducted. Morris also ill-advisedly encouraged Michael Chamberlain to participate in a phone interview with an Adelaide reporter, before the Chamberlains had the benefit of legal advice.

Inspector Gilroy and Sergeant Lincoln arrived late on the day after Azaria vanished, and the talkative Lincoln soon confided his feelings of scepticism about the case to both Gilroy and an Adelaide reporter named de Luca. Lincoln, after spending only minimal time at the crime scene, prematurely offered the opinion that Azaria Chamberlain was the victim of foul play. He added that a dingo could not be a culprit, as it would be too small to carry a ten pound baby in its mouth.

By then the general public was taking a keen interest in initial media reports about the disappearance and many supported the view that a dingo would not attack a human being. Elements of the tabloid press incorrectly divulged that the literal meaning of the name "Azaria" was "sacrifice in the desert". This revelation indicated to some, that the parents were guilty of a heinous crime against their own baby. It also became known that Michael Chamberlain was an ordained minister of the little known Seventh Day Adventist Church; this new information added to a growing distrust about the Chamberlain's beliefs and lifestyle.

Back in Alice Springs, police dwelt on a series of puzzling questions about the Azaria case. Why were there only small amounts of blood on the jump suit that the baby was wearing at the time of the alleged attack? Why had the baby's matinee jacket not been discovered in nearby bushland? The general uncertainty resulted in Detective Sergeant Graeme Charlswood taking command of the case, but the Chamberlains were not informed about Charlswood's appointment before they returned home to Michael's church pastoral duties in Mt Isa.

Consequently, Lindy was surprised when a new police officer arrived at her door step and requested formal statements from all family members about the chain of events in the Uluru car park in the past month. The confused woman believed she had already provided such information and at that stage she had no idea she was a suspect in the unsolved case.

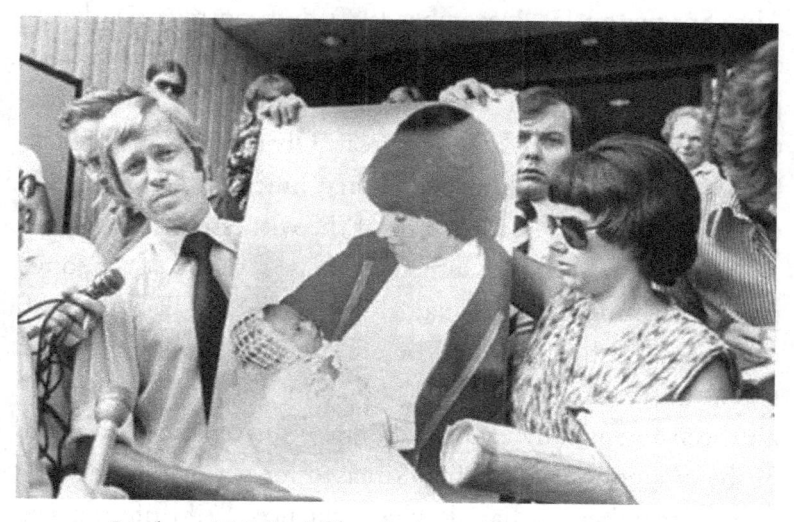

Lindy and Michael Chamberlin with a photo of Azaria

Charlswood, despite secretly taping Lindy's information, allegedly did not provide her with an official caution before an interview commenced, nor did he give her the option of having legal representation. During the exhaustive questioning session Constable Morris, the accompanying investigator, noted the mother's distress when her missing child's clothing was presented. He asked that the investigation be put briefly on hold, so that the woman could regain her composure. Charlswood ignored the request and continued to question Lindy. Later, when Michael Chamberlain was questioned, he received an officially caution before the interview began.

Next morning headlines in some national daily newspapers declared that a dingo did not kill Azaria Chamberlain. To support their claims, forensic evidence was cited, evidence that Lindy and Michael Chamberlain would have been privy to only hours before the general public was informed. It seemed the media was being kept more up to date with developments, than the prime suspects in the case.

An inquest headed by Coroner Denis Barrett began in Alice Springs on 15th December 1980, and controversial developments continued to surface. Barrett was forced to correct perceptions of media bias during proceedings and Lindy Chamberlain received a death threat. Disturbingly, before the inquest was adjourned until February, much of the police evidence had been refuted by some of the witnesses.

After the hearing resumed, it was revealed that some police personnel involved had ill advisedly handled items of the missing baby's clothing, before official photographs were taken. Furthermore, alleged blood stains in the tent area had not been forensically examined. These discrepancies resulted in the NT police force being criticised for permitting inexperienced members to handle vital evidence. Wild life rangers were also admonished for allowing the Uluru area to become potentially dangerous for tourists.

Coroner Barrett delivered his judgement on 20th February. He concluded that, "after her death, the body of Azaria Chamberlain was taken from the possession of a dingo, and disposed of by an unknown method, by a person or persons unknown".

The mystifying case remained "live". Seven months after Barrett's coronial judgement, Operation Ochre, a recently formed NT police task force, visited Lindy and Michael Chamberlain at their new residence at Gooranbong near Newcastle. Detective Sergeant Charlswood produced search certificates. He then informed the couple that Paul Everingham, the NT Chief Minister, had authorised further investigations being conducted because new evidence had become available since the Barrett inquest concluded. Consequently, police applied to the NT Supreme Court to have the coronial findings quashed.

On this occasion the Chamberlains refused to be interviewed, but this did not deter the task force from packing up several possessions that had accompanied the family to Alice Springs in 1980, including the family car. If legal advice had been sought about the confiscation of the car, removal may have been refused.

Operation Ochre personnel had unexpected company during their visit. Shortly after officers knocked on the Chamberlain's front door at Gooranbong, media personnel arrived by helicopter and other forms of transport at the tiny settlement The "media invasion" further confirmed that news outlets were better informed about ongoing developments than the Chamberlains themselves.

A lengthy second inquest began on 14th December 1981,

and on 2nd February 1982 a different finding was reached. On this occasion the coroner concluded that circumstantial evidence supported accusations of child murder against Lindy and Michael Chamberlain.

The coroner believed that the baby had been killed in the family car. Then, while a search was being conducted for the missing child, the couple probably hid the small body in Michael Chamberlain's camera case. The couple then allegedly removed Azaria's clothing from her body and placed these garments in a location where they would be easily found by a search party. The body of the baby was presumed to have been buried in a place unknown.

Lindy Chamberlain was subsequently charged with murder, while her husband was accused of being an accessory after the fact. Bail for each of the accused was set at $5,000 and an April court hearing was set.

The trial date was actually changed until September, partly because Lindy had become pregnant. The couple declared that the birth of a new baby had been planned for some time, but sceptical members of the media and general public voiced opinions that the baby had been deliberately conceived, in order to gain sympathy from jury members.

"The trial of the century" began in Darwin before Mr Justice James Muirhead on 13th September 1982. From the outset the Crown claimed that significant scientific evidence existed, which proved that Azaria died after having her throat cut with scissors. Furthermore, in the family car, blood spots had been found that contradicted any notion that a dingo had killed the baby.

In the early stages of the trial, Justice Muirhead delivered statements that indicated he was unconvinced about Lindy Chamberlain being unfairly interrogated by Detective

Sergeant Charlswood. At the end of the exhaustive trial, His Honour delivered a two day address to the jury, before guilty verdicts were reached. Muirhead then committed Lindy Chamberlain to life imprisonment for "as long as she will live" for the murder of her baby daughter. Michael Chamberlain received a more lenient sentence—a suspended 18 month sentence and three years probation.

Authorities also made decisions about parental access to the new baby. The mother was only allowed to be with her child for an hour after giving birth and no visitations between mother and child were permitted for a further 12 months. Kahlia Chamberlain was born on 17th November 1982; by then Lindy's quest for a new trial had begun to gather momentum.

The "Free Lindy" campaign, which was largely financed by the Seventh Day Adventist Church, became one of the best organised public campaigns ever seen in Australia, and it concentrated on legal, scientific and popular issues.

The promotions included national rallies, numerous door knocks and comprehensive advertising, with Sally Lowe and other sympathisers present at the Uluru campground drama, featuring strongly in the campaign.

The Crown had relied heavily on the forensic findings of Joy Kuhl at Lindy's Darwin trial, but the opinions of this previously well-regarded expert began to be disputed. New evidence suggested that the stains found in the Chamberlain's car were not drops of blood, but seepage from sound-deadener. Practical tests also indicated that dogs or dingoes could cut as well as tear through fabric, so the damage to the child's jump suit could indeed have been caused by canine teeth rather than scissors. Some of the hair samples on the baby's clothing appeared to be from a dingo. Other stains found in the car were not haemoglobin based; they were alleged to be copper dust from the Mt Isa mines, near where the Chamberlains then lived.

The case was re-opened on 29th April 1983, but Justice Jenkinson, Justice Bowen and Justice Forster unanimously upheld the previous verdict. They found there was no evidence to support the dingo attack theory and fully supported Ms Kuhl's claims.

Lindy Chamberlain remained in Berrimal Prison. She applied for temporary release on compassionate grounds when her son Reagan became hospitalised after suffering a serious eye injury. This wish was finally granted "on procedural grounds" after long delays from the NT government. Lindy was also denied legal aide for her High Court case.

The High Court again rejected an appeal, but on this occasion there was cause for future optimism. The result was a split decision, with two of the five judges supporting her case. At the time rumours circulated that the NT Solicitor General had canvassed the possibility of a pardon being granted if the "Free Lindy" campaign ended and if Lindy Chamberlain changed her plea to "guilty". Any possibility of agreement on this issue was rejected by the Chamberlains.

Finally crucial new evidence destroyed the Crown's case. On 2nd February 1986, a search party looking for the missing climber David Brett, unexpectedly discovered a baby's matinee jacket partially buried in the sand at the base of Uluru. It was only metres away from where items of clothing belonging to Azaria Chamberlain had been discovered in 1980. Three days later her mother identified the newly found garment as being the very one her daughter wore on the night she disappeared.

On 7th February the NT Government stated that Lindy Chamberlain had "suffered enough" and she was released from custody. Chief Minister Paul Everingham, who had been touted by some as having a promising future in Federal politics, quit public life altogether and opened a legal practice. Other prominent members of the existing government resigned their portfolios and the Chamberlains were granted the right to face the Court of Criminal Appeals, to have their convictions quashed.

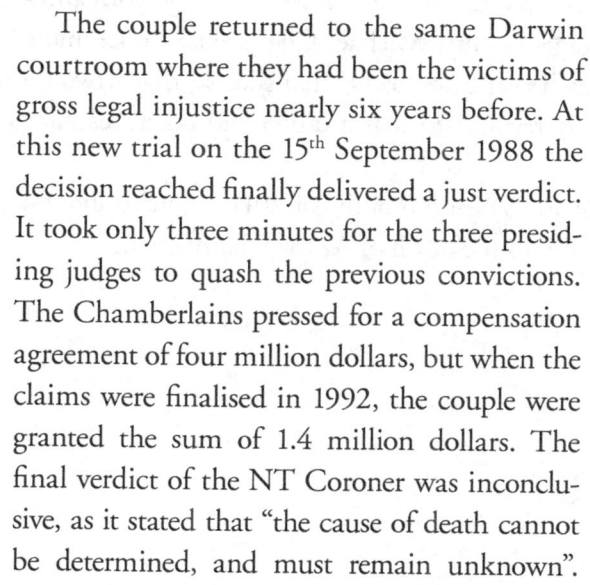

Lindy Chamberlain today.

The couple returned to the same Darwin courtroom where they had been the victims of gross legal injustice nearly six years before. At this new trial on the 15th September 1988 the decision reached finally delivered a just verdict. It took only three minutes for the three presiding judges to quash the previous convictions. The Chamberlains pressed for a compensation agreement of four million dollars, but when the claims were finalised in 1992, the couple were granted the sum of 1.4 million dollars. The final verdict of the NT Coroner was inconclusive, as it stated that "the cause of death cannot be determined, and must remain unknown".

Lindy was free at last, but both Michael and she continued to confront problems. She became Lindy Chamberlain-Creighton after first divorcing and later re-marrying, while Michael Chamberlain resigned as a Seventh Day Adventist minister.

Since then there have been documented instances of dingo attacks in Australia. On Fraser Island, off the Central Queensland coast, the long heard rumours about dingo aggression became tragically credible, when a small boy died in early 2001 after being savaged in a local camp ground.

The death occurred nearly a decade after the anguished cry of "a dingo took my baby" was heard ringing through an outback desert, but the claims of an innocent mother were further vindicated.

Despite evidence to the contrary, the cause of Azaria's death is still officially listed as "unknown". However, on the 30th anniversary of the tragic fatality, Michael Chamberlain once more called for the death certificate to be changed, so that it would finally be officially recognised that a dingo had taken his baby daughter's life.

Consequently, in the early months of 2011, a fourth inquest may be conducted into the death of Azaria Chamberlain.

AN UNSOLVED MYSTERY

In July 2004, Bradley John Murdoch received a life sentence for the murder of Peter Falconio, but contentious issues continue to surface in this mystifying case.

It became a controversial situation after the 28-year-old English tourist vanished in Australia's vast and lonely outback on 14th July 2000. Over a decade has past, but Falconio's body has still not been found. Furthermore, no weapon has been discovered and no known motive for the crime has been established.

All available evidence appeared to be circumstantial in nature, before forensic tests were conducted on Falconio's girlfriend's stained T-shirt, as well as the steering wheel of the Kombi van in which the couple were travelling. The DNA evidence uncovered supposedly matched a sample provided by the accused man. This was probably a persuasive factor for the Darwin jury, which found Bradley Murdoch guilty of both murdering Peter Falconio and abducting and assaulting Joanne Lees.

A sensational new twist surfaced about similar forensic evidence in December 2007. The same DNA test, which secured a verdict against Murdoch, was ruled inadmissible in an unrelated case in Britain because it was deemed to be unreliable. No definite ruling was made about this possible UK precedent,

Bradley John Murdoch

when this book went to print. Murdoch has currently lodged two appeals against his conviction, but the High Court rejected both attempts.

Falconio and his 27-year-old English girlfriend came to Australia on an extended holiday in the year 2000. They spent some time in Sydney before purchasing a second hand orange Kombi van in which they intended to explore more remote parts of the country. Around 4pm on 14th July, the couple began their long trip to the Alice Springs area, where their dream holiday suddenly became a nightmare.

The young couple had shared a joint of cannabis, while they enjoyed an outback sunset near the Ti Tree Roadhouse, before they continued their journey up the lonely Sturt Highway. Lees later confided that she felt threatened by their extreme isolation, which is why she persuaded her lover not to stop and extinguish a few small spot fires that were burning near the roadside.

Then, around 7.30-8pm, it is alleged a fast moving vehicle suddenly appeared behind them. When it drew alongside, the driver gestured urgently towards the back of the Kombi van. Visibility at the time was poor, but Lees was later able to provide a detailed description of the man's appearance. She was also remembered details about a dog that sat next to the driver.

Peter Falconio was supposedly concerned that sparks might be flying from the rear of their old van, so he ignored Lees' misgivings about the stranger and pulled to a halt. After he joined the man at the rear of the van, he asked Lees to press her foot on the accelerator a few times. At first Lees presumed that the explosions she then heard were backfires from the old vehicle. That mundane explanation changed abruptly, however, when the stranger allegedly appeared at the driver's window and menacingly pointed a silver revolver at her head.

The assailant tied Lees' hands behind her with some home made handcuffs, before allegedly striking the struggling young woman and shoving her into his vehicle next to his dog. Before he thrust a canvas bag over her head, the anguished woman allegedly cried, "Are you going to rape me? Have you shot my boyfriend?"

"No," was the curt answer from the attacker, whom Lee later described as being of medium build and wearing a black cap. After she was placed in the back of the stranger's white utility, Joanne Lees managed to free herself from the bag. She then believes she heard the sound of something being dragged through the nearby gravel on the side of the highway.

Lees fell heavily onto the side of the road, after she tumbled herself off the tray of the utility. The still handcuffed woman managed to dash into the scrub adjoining the highway and hid under a small bush. She recalls the cursing stranger using a torch to search for her in the darkness, before he abandoned the

Joanne Lees and Peter Falconio just before their trip to Alice Springs

brief hunt. He then drove the Kombi van a short distance away from the crime scene and departed in his own vehicle.

The traumatised young woman remained in hiding for a considerable time, not trusting the sound of a few other vehicles passing along the nearby highway, in case it signalled her assailant was returning. It was possibly hours later before she heard the welcome sound of a heavy road train approaching. The still handcuffed Joanne Lees then ran to the side of the road and waved her arms frantically to attract the driver's attention.

Vince Miller was at the wheel of the truck. The startled man applied the brakes as soon as he saw Ms Lees and managed to bring the huge vehicle to a stop about a kilometre further on. Miller feared he may have driven over her, and began anxiously searching for a body after jumping out of the driver's cabin. It was a very relieved man who soon came across the sobbing Lees calling for help near the now stationary road train. Miller and his co-driver Rodney Brown cut her handcuffs free and attempted to calm the almost hysterical woman.

However, when Lees revealed there was a man somewhere in the darkness who had shot her boyfriend, the pair quickly decided not to search for an alleged missing person. They drove the shaken woman back to safe refuge at the Barrow Creek Hotel and from there Alice Springs police were contacted. An investigating team arrived approximately three hours later.

It took only a short time for frictions to emerge between Lees, the NT police officers investigating the crime and the national media. The young English woman appeared to find questions put to her to be both intrusive and annoying, and she began to show a reluctance to cooperate in interview sessions. They in turn were disturbed by Lees' constant complaints about their inability to find the missing Peter, her perceived need for personal privacy and her initial refusal to communicate with her parents in England. In this growing atmosphere of mutual mistrust, many unanswered questions began to surface.

Why were there so many discrepancies in Joanne Lees' evidence? How did she avoid being recaptured when she was only hiding behind a low bush and her alleged attacker was searching for her with a torch? Why didn't he use his dog in the search? Why were her wounds only superficial, when she had supposedly been punched around the head before falling heavily on the roadside? What was the motive behind the alleged killing and abduction? If Peter Falconio was now deceased, where was his body? Why was there no sign of spatter blood from the alleged close range shots? Was the missing Englishman actually still alive?

Joanne Lees at the Supreme Court, Darwin

Questions were also asked about the commitment Lees had to her long term de facto relationship, after it was discovered she had a brief affair with an English backpacker when Falconio and she were living together in Sydney. Some observers wondered if the young couple and their alleged assailant had previously met before the attack took place. It was also surprising that Lees described her attacker as being "of average height" when it later became patently obvious that Bradley Murdoch was a very tall and powerfully built man.

Public interest in the case rose in intensity after two credible witnesses claimed they saw Peter Falconio eight days after his alleged disappearance. Teacher aide Robert Brown and his partner Melissa Kendall (a future assistant registrar in their home town of Bourke) both claimed they saw Falconio with three other adults at a petrol station in Bourke. The group supposedly drove off together in a green utility, but an immediate search was not activated, as police were not notified about the possible sighting until next day. By then the group had apparently vanished into a remote area of the vast outback and no trace of them ever surfaced. Around that time there were also less convincing reports about Falconio being spotted in both Terrigal and Mt Isa, towns hundreds of kilometres apart.

From Joanne Lees' recollections, an identikit photograph of a long haired suspect with a droopy moustache were compiled and widely circulated. At first there was no worthwhile public response, but on 16th May 2002, police investigations received a much needed boost, after James Hepi was arrested near his South Australian property with three kilograms of cannabis in his possession. Hepi was convinced that his co-drug runner, Bradley John Murdoch, had "dobbed" on him to the police. Consequently, he volunteered information about Murdoch's supposed link with the Peter Falconio case.

Previously, Murdoch had allegedly boasted to Hepi that he could dispose of a body in the outback and that the remains would never be found. By then, police had become curious about why Murdoch had drastically changed both his appearance and the design of his white utility after he returned to his Broome home. Further investigations revealed that Bradley John Murdoch had a violent past.

In May 1995, he was sentenced to 21 months in gaol after firing several shots near a group of aborigines at Fitzroy Crossing. The confrontation at gunpoint resulted from a recent argument, but luckily no casualties occurred. On that occasion, Murdoch voluntarily surrendered himself to police soon after the incident took place.

On 28th August 2002, Bradley John Murdoch was arrested at gunpoint by police outside a supermarket in Port Augusta. Blood samples were obtained from the suspect. Later, on 10th October, investigators reported that Murdoch's DNA matched the samples from the blood drops previously discovered on Joanne Lees' shirt and the steering wheel of the Kombi van.

Bradley John Murdoch faced accusations of murder and abduction, but a much awaited trial was delayed while the accused faced other unrelated charges for the abduction and rape of a mother and her 12-year-old daughter in South Australia. Murdoch was ultimately cleared of all charges in this case, but police apprehended him immediately after the state court reached its decision. He was then transferred to the Darwin Remand Centre, from where he faced future committal proceedings in the Falconio case.

The trial began on 17th May 2004. Joanne Lees was the chief Crown witness and family members of Peter Falconio also travelled from England for the much publicised event.

The accused pleaded not guilty. He denied handcuffing Lees and he was unable to explain how his DNA matched the incriminating blood stains. Murdoch's defence barrister attempted to cast doubts about the credibility of both Hepi and Lees as witnesses. It was also intimated that police tampered with evidence to gain the DNA result they needed for an arrest.

Eighty-five witnesses gave evidence and 350 exhibits were viewed in the exhaustive eight-week trial before the jury finally found Bradley John Murdoch guilty of all charges. He received a life sentence, with a non-parole period of 28 years.

Murdoch continues to maintain his innocence, but by June 2007 the Australian High Court rejected what appeared to be his last opportunity to appeal. Nevertheless other issues arising from the case have continued to surface.

In early December of that year, *The Age* reported that Murdoch was poised to use the conduct of the NT's Chief Magistrate as a trigger to have his case re-opened. Joanne Martin, the daughter of Chief Magistrate Brian Martin, gave birth to a baby whose father had links with Murdoch's court case.

An alleged conflict of interests appeared plausible, but this possibility lost momentum after the Chief Magistrate claimed there was nothing legally improper about any aspects of his daughter's relationship. The NT Legal Aid Commission agreed that the couple had not met until well after the completion of Murdoch's trial, which effectively ended Murdoch's hopes.

Previously, when Bradley Murdoch sought a gaol transfer to be near his aging mother in WA, the NT police offered to accommodate his wish, if he revealed the whereabouts of Peter Falconio's body.

"How can I tell them where the body is, when I don't know?" has been Murdoch's consistent response.

The twists and turns of this mystifying outback case continues to fascinate the Australian public.

BIBLIOGRAPHY

De Vries, Susanna: *Great Pioneer Women of the Outback*, Harper Collins Publications, 2005.

Ferguson, Ian: *Murders That Shocked Australia*, Brolga Publishing Pty. Ltd., 2007.

Ferguson, Ian: *Crimes That Shocked Australia*, Brolga Publishing Pty. Ltd., 2008.

Gascoine, John: *Nuggets-Golden and Human*, Brolga Publishing Pty. Ltd., 2001.

Lewis, Wendy: *See Australia and Die: Tales of Misadventure Down Under.* New Holland Australia, 2007.

Mortimer, Malcolm: *The History of Wonnangatta Station*, Spectrum Publications, 1961.

My Country. Australian Poetry and Short Stories: Two Hundred Years, (selected by Leonie Kramer), Ure Smith Press, 1985.

Pollard, Jack: *The Horse Tamer*, Rigby Books, 1978.

Ramsland, John & Mooney Christopher: *Remembering Aboriginal Heroes*, Brolga Publishing Pty. Ltd., 2006.

Simpson, Bruce: *Hell, Highwater and Hard Cases*, ABC Books, Sydney, 1999.

INDEX

A

ABC 16, 122, 161
Aboriginal Deaths in Custody 162
Afghan camel trains 47
Air Medical Service 125-26
Ammo 90
Aranda Arts Council 190
ARIA awards 184
Army Survey Corps 138
Arnhem Land 180, 186, 199-200
Ashley, Miriam 200
ASTIC 119, 153
Atherton Tablelands 110-11
Australia Day 4, 200, 215
Australian Infantry Force 70, 175
Australia Zoo 213
Ayers Rock 215, 236

B

Baird, Jean 127
Bandar, Faith 115-6
Banks, Joseph 3
Barrallier, Francis 6
Barrett, Denis Coroner 240-41
Bates, Daisy 112-4
Bates, Jack 113
Batterbee, Rex 190
Bauer, Gladys 91-2
Beadell, Len 138-40
Beagle Bay Mission 113, 116
Binstead, Joe 145, 147-8
Birdsville Cup 49
Birdsville Motor Museum 88
Birdsville Track 87

Bjelke Petersen, Sir Joh 143
Blackwood, Kathleen 39
Blanasi, David 180
Blaxland, Gregory 65, 6-7
Blue Lake leap 56
Boer War 112, 172
Bogucki, Robert 221-3
Bohning, Elsie 93
Bonner, Neville 158, 160-1
Bonney, Charles 76-7
Botany Bay 3-4, 115
Boulton, Bert 64
Bowers, Shaun 205-6
Boyd, Arthur 194
Boyden, Captain Rex 145
Bradman, Don 51, 147
Bradshaw, Atalanta 98, 123
Bradshaw, Doris 98
Bradshaw, Mortimore 98
Bradshaw, Thomas 98
Brendt, Bertha 169
Brett, David 215-6, 244
Brisbane Country Week 178
British Empire Medal 140
British-Australian Telegraph Company 78,
Brown, Robert 252
Brown, Rodney 250
Bryce, Annie 61
Bryers, Isabella 170
Burgess, Charles 148
Burke and Wills initiative 15
Burrup, Eddie 44
Butler, Harry 161

C

Canning, Alfred 82-6
Chamberlain, Azaria 215-6, 236-46
Chamberlain, Kahlia 243
Chamberlain, Lindy 209, 216, 236-7, 239-45
Chamberlain, Michael 236-43, 245-6
Chamberlain, Reagan 237, 244
Charlswood, Detective Sergeant Graeme 239-40, 243
Churchill Fellowship 153
Cobden, Mary Jane 36-7
Companion of the British Empire 114
Cook, Captain James 2-3
Coolgardie safes 41
Corkel, Scarlett 209
Cyclone Althea 232
Cyclone Larry 231-2
Cyclone Mahina 231
Cyclone Tracy 233-35

D

Dampier, William 1-2
Darcy, Jimmy 123-4
Darwin Cup 49
Department of Aboriginal Affairs 72, 122
Dodson, Mick 162-3
Dodson, Patrick 163
Dreamtime 32, 154, 200
Drysdale, Sir George Russell 192-3
Durack, Elizabeth 43
Durack, Mary 42-3, 103
Durack, Patsy 41, 43
Durack, Peter 44
Dwyer, Margaret 112

E

Eddie Kocki Mabo Library 156
Egan, Ted 72-3
Endeavour 2
Evans, Evelyn "Evie" 33, 123, 109-11
Evans, George 6
Evans, Tim 110
Everingham, Paul 241, 245

F

Falconio, Peter 247-54
Fifth Light Horse Regiment 175
First Fleet 41
Flying Sisters 1265
Flynn, Reverend John 103, 124-9
Forrest, Andrew 159
Forrest, Baron John 27-30
Free Lindy campaign 243-4
Froth and Bubble Festival 56
Fuller, Geoff 222

G

Gage, Clinton 209-10
Gage, Dylan 209-10
Gage, Ross 209-10
Gardner, John 190
Generation One 159
Gibbs, Pearl 115
Gibson, Alfred 139
Glandberger, Jennifer 209
Goeschka, Karl 219-20
Goodsell, Briony 201-2
Great Depression 126, 135, 177

259

Great Lakes system 10
Great War 135, 172
Grossmueler, Gabriele 219-20
Gulf of Carpentaria 14, 20-1, 25, 71, 133, 232
Gulpilil, David 199-200
Gulpilil, Jamie 200
Gun Barrel Highway 140, 217
Gunn, Aeneas 69, 158-9, 182
Gunn, Jeannie 69, 159, 161, 163

H

Hancock Prospecting Company 143-4
Hancock, Lang 141-44
Hanson, Pauline 196
Harney, Bill 70-1
Harpur, Charles 166
Harris, Rolf 64, 180
Hawdon, Joseph 75-7
Heidi group 194
Hepi, James 252-3
Herbig, Catherine 36
Hermannsburg Mission 94, 189, 190-1
Hethering, Ethel 224-5
Heysen, Hans 100
Heysen, Nora 100
Hia Ono, Masa 217-8
High Court of Australia 32, 156
Hiroshima 234
Hovell Tree 8
Hovell, William 8
Howard, John 120, 158
Howard, Nancy 48
Hughes, Billy 170
Hume, Hamilton 8-10
Hunter, Ruby 181, 183-5

I

Idriess, Ion Llewellyn "Jack" 175-6
Iolanthe 71
Irwin, Bindi 212-13
Irwin, Bob 213
Irwin, Steve 211-3
Irwin, Terri 213

J

Jeffrey, Steve 89-90
Johannsen, Ottile 94-5
John Eyre, Edward 17-19
Jones, Ignatius 90
Jordan, Isabel von 203-4

K

Kanakas 95
Kellaway, Stuart 186
Kelly, Paul 181-2, 184, 187
Kendall, Henry 56, 166
Kendall, Melissa 252
Kennedy, Edward 14, 22
Kenny, Rhelma 146, 149
Kerr, Andrew 207-8
Kerr, Diane 207-8
Kidman, Sir Sidney 58, 102-3, 132-5, 137
Kruze, Tom 87-8
Kuhl, Joy 243-4
Kuppers, Christopher 220

L

Lady Julianna 5
Laiwanga, Djoli 180
Lands Right Treaty 153
Lang, Jack 170
Langford, Sandy 89-90

Lawson, Henry 1, 35-6, 91-2, 168-72, 196
Lawson, Louisa Albury 168
Lawson, Peter 168
Lawson, William 6-7, 65
Lees, Joanne 247-54
Leichardt, Ludwig 20-1, 27
Lindsay Gordon, Adam 55-6
Lindsay's leap 56
Lowe, Sally 236-37, 243
Loy, Granny Lum 95-6
Luhmann, Baz 200

M

Mabo 32
Mabo, Eddie 155-6
Mackellar, Dorothea 173-4
Macquarie, Governor Lachlan 5
Madden, Madeleine 159
Maguire, Dorothy 48
Mann, Brett 205-6
Marshall, Beryl 177
Marshall, Charlee 176-7
Martin, Chief Magistrate Brian 254
Martin-Kieser, Hans 220
Maunsell, Charlie 109-11
Maunsell, Ronald 110
McCallum, Elizabeth 38
McDouall Stuart, John 15-6, 24, 78, 80
McGough, Ashley 205-6
Meckering earthquake 229-230
Melbourne Cup 70
Miethke, Miss Adelaide 46
Miles Franklin Award 21
Miller, Jessie 38
Miller, Vince 250
Mitchell, Thelma 136
Mitchell, Sir Thomas 13-4, 22, 76

Monk, Ngarla Kunoth 121-2
Morris, Eta 176
Muirhead, Justice James 242-43
Murdoch, Bradley John 247-8, 251-4
Murdoch, Rupert 89

N

Namatjira, Albert 189-91
National Reconciliation Council 72
National Trust of Australia 72
Nobel Prize for Literature 21
Nolan, Sir Sidney 194-5
Nullarbor Plain 17-8, 27, 29

O

O'Brien, John 62
O'Hara Burke, Robert 23-6
O'Reilly, Bernard 146-9
O'Sullivan, Charlene 201-2
One Nation 196
One People of Australia League 161
Oodnadatta Nursing Hostel 125
Order of Australia 74, 119, 141, 162, 193
Order of the British Empire 108, 126, 173
Ord River Irrigation Scheme 43
Overland Telegraph line 16, 27, 78-81, 134

P

Parker, Catherine "Katie" Langloh 99-100
Partridge, Kingsley 127
Paterson, Grace 172

Paterson, Hugh, 172
Pearl Harbour 227
pedal radio 125
Percival, John 194
Phillip, Arthur 5
Proud, John 145, 147-8

Q

Queen's Coronation Medal 190

R

Rabbit Proof Fence 64, 82, 86, 200
Redford, Henry Arthur "Harry" 68-9
Radford, Ron 192
Randolph Stow, Percival 100
Rankin, Dame Isabelle 161
Red Lancer 56
Reed, John 194
Reed, Sunday 194
Riley, Jack 89, 91, 93-4
Rinehart, Gina 141, 143-4
Rio Tinto Company 142
Riotinto, Cenzink 154
Roach, Archie 181, 183-5
Robless, Glen 203-4
Roff, Derek 236
Ross, John 78-81
Rothwell, James 204
Rowles, Kasey 209
Royal Flying Doctor Service 44, 46, 103, 126, 127
Royal Geographical Society 19
Rumbularah Mission 183

S

School of The Air 45-6

Singer sewing machine 42
Singh, Jundah 47
Singh, Roddah 47
Skuthorpe, Lance 85, 87, 89
Sorohan, Alicia 207-8
Sorohan, Bill 207
South Seas voyage 3
St Clair, Garrison 222
Steele, Mary 92
Stinson crash 145-9
Stolen Generation 120, 150, 184, 201
Streeton, Major-General Alan 234
Sturt, Charles 9-12, 15
Sydney Olympic 89, 187

T

Tamworth Country Music Festival 177
Tamworth Fireside Festival 177
Tea and Sugar train 29
Tent Embassy 152, 158
Terra Nullius 31, 155-6
Tierney, Elizabeth 97
Timor Sea 227
Todd Regatta 49
Traeger, Alfred 125, 128-9
Trans Australian Railway 29-30
Tribal Council 118
Tucker, Albert 194
Tudawali, Robert 121, 198-9
Tyson, James 130-1

U

Uluru 71, 215-6, 224, 236, 241, 244
United Aborigines Mission 119

W

Walker, Alice Emily 172
Walker, Bruce 117
Waters, Andrew 204
Wave Hill Cricket Club 49-50
Wentworth, William 6-7, 75
Wentworth, William Charles 165-6
Western Front 70
Westray, Jim 145, 147-8
White, Alan 102
White, Cornelius "Con" 101-3
White, Doris 101
White, Gary 102
White, Myrtle 101-4, 107, 123
Whitlam, Gough 158
Wilson, John 6, 65-6
Withnell, Emma 97
Woomera Rocket Range 138-9
World War I 29, 70, 100, 108, 110, 125, 135, 172
World War II 92, 103, 111, 117, 139, 143, 194, 227, 234
Wright, Isobel 134
Wright, Peter 142
Wylie, 17-8, 27

Y

Yothu Yindi, 181, 186-8
Young, Peter 49-50
Yunupingu, Galarrwuy 186
Yunupingu, Mandawuy 186-7

Z

Zahmel, Jeff 212

Order

OUTBACK STORIES
Ian Ferguson

ISBN 978-1-925367-05-8

Qty

RRP AU$24.99 .....

Postage within Australia AU$5.00 .....

TOTAL* $_____

* All prices include GST

Name:..

Address: ....

....

Phone:...

Email: ....

Payment: ❏ Money Order ❏ Cheque ❏ MasterCard ❏ Visa

Cardholder's Name:..

Credit Card Number: ....

Signature:...

Expiry Date: ....

Allow 7 days for delivery.

Payment to: Marzocco Consultancy (ABN 14 067 257 390)
PO Box 12544
A'Beckett Street, Melbourne, 8006
Victoria, Australia
admin@brolgapublishing.com.au

Be Published

Publish through a successful publisher.
Brolga Publishing is represented through:
- **National** book trade distribution, including sales, marketing & distribution through **Macmillan Australia**.
- **International** book trade distribution to
    - The United Kingdom
    - North America
    - Sales representation in South East Asia
- **Worldwide e-Book distribution**

For details and inquiries, contact:
Brolga Publishing Pty Ltd
PO Box 12544
A'Beckett St VIC 8006

Phone: 0414 608 494
markzocchi@brolgapublishing.com.au
ABN: 46 063 962 443
(Email for a catalogue request)